1

The Knowledge

Das Wissen

My heart is a garden called Eden

JENS BEHRMANN

The Knowledge

Das Wissen

First Edition
First English edition

ISBN: 978-3-00-039771-4

"The connection to our inner voice is the foundation for a life of satisfaction, inner peace and unimaginable happiness"

Dedication

It is with a deep sense of gratitude that I would like to dedicate this book to you. May it benefit all those who are ready to be inspired, on their journey and on their respective paths through life. It is my intention that you may find out more about life and its essential principles.

We are all subject to these universal principles, there are no exceptions; so let us find out more about forming our own meanings and our own realizations about these universal principles.

The "Knowledge" within can open all the doors of our understanding and then it begins to apply these principles to our daily lives. "The Knowledge" is a key without exception, to help everyone unlock the treasure of infinite wisdom, in all areas of our lives.

In this book you will find the keys within you that you need, so that „The Knowledge" can become evident in your own life.

Jens Behrmann

CONTENTS

CONTENTS

CONTENTS

Thank you

I wish to offer my thanks to all those who have ever met me, whilst on my life's journey. It is through these meetings and relationships that have made it possible for me to write this book. The lessons that we have offered to each other, have been at times very profound and not always easy, while at other times, joyful and loving.

But they were always inspiring.

I have learned that all of those things that I sought for on the outside, are available from within myself, and that everything that I have encountered has been, and always is in accordance, with my feelings, thoughts and actions. Thus it has been possible for me, to gain a new perception of my life, to accept that other people are not responsible for my circumstances, and to consciously find the Divine and infinite being within me. This I call 'The Knowledge'. The wisdom contained within is universal, in that it can assist and serve each one of us, if we are willing.

With love and gratitude, *Jens*

What is "The Knowledge"?

"The Knowledge" is the recognition of the principles at work in the entire universe that also apply to us.

When we find a way to this universal and infinite knowledge, we have the opportunity to achieve things in our lives that once seemed impossible.

The " Knowledge" gives us the understanding that it is far more important to set our focus on the inner world than on the outer world of delusion. Everyone contains this inner wisdom within themselves and they can find ways to reconnect with it. We often unconsciously move away from this knowledge, acting out of fear which comes from our ego minds and from our personality.

"The Knowledge" shows us clearly, that it comes in different forms to everyone. Many of us understand it as our consciousness, something that we already know; we just have to wake up to it, consciously. We know it to be the Truth. Everybody can access this „Knowledge". It is in every one of us. It can inspire us to be guided by a wiser and deeper understanding; it can take us to greater happiness, joy and prosperity in all areas of lives.

Let "The Knowledge" guide you on your path to your true self.

Foreword

Just as we learn about the physical world from the education and guidance provided by our parents, siblings and teachers, and maybe later by our own efforts, we should also continue to learn and grow spiritually. If we continue to develop in one area of our life only, we will never know how many different facts there are to our lives. I was extremely fortunate in having a profound experience showing me what the feelings of love and unity are like in a different state of consciousness.

The love we feel for each other is often characterized by fears that relate to experiences and expectations from the past. Who is really free in his thinking and feelings? We are all characterized by painful losses and the fear of losing each other. This often obscures our view of who we and other people really are. This is rooted in our personalities and our habits. Our personalities should be as clear as a sparkling diamond. This would allow more light, with all its brightness, its whole color spectrum and its infinite wisdom, to become visible in our thinking, our feelings and actions, and in our words. When this happens, we begin to live the loving wisdom that exists within each and every one of us. This book aims at providing a modest of contribution towards enabling people to find a way out of the trials and tribulations of their lives and helps them to move towards clarity, inner peace and more power and love for each other. I want to emphasize that I respect all belief systems and philosophies that aim at leading people, through non-violence and through consideration of each person's free will, on the path to greater self-determination and more love and peace towards each other.

How my journey began

As long as I can remember, I always had a sense of foreboding; as so many people too. As a small boy, of 5 years old, I had a wart in my forefinger. I remember a woman neighbor, to whom I went from time to time to receive a small piece of chocolate. She asked me on that day, do you want the wart to disappear? I said, yes, to which she replied, so do it.... She advised me that I should pick up a stone and touch the wart with this stone 3 times, while saying loudly, "In the name of the Father, the Son and the Holy Spirit. Then I should put the stone back to the place where I had taken it from. I did as I was told. Three days later the miracle happened. The wart was completely gone. Thus this knowledge came to me at a very early age. Nevertheless, I had other plans, and didn't look at it again.

So the years passed. At age 13 I had a very dramatic experience. I often went with on a tour my father. He was a truck driver and I would travel with him. I remember that my mother always had an uneasy feeling, a fear that we might have an accident. She would always say, "drive carefully". Mothers often worry, but on this day however, her fear was confirmed. It was March and still cold but dry. After the truck was loaded, we drove off. We reached the destination for that evening and the goods were unloaded. Everything went as usual. Once we got back on the highway, we wanted to overtake a truck.

When changing lanes, it happened. We hit black ice, the 30ton truck began to skid, we collided into the left guardrail and I heard a loud bang. I jumped from the front passenger seat to the sleeping cabin and lay down there. The truck slammed into in the right guardrail. Then again, an impact on the other side.

My head bumped hard against the cabin wall. Then the journey ended abruptly as we hit hard into a bridge pillar, of which there were only a few every couple of kilometers. I lost consciousness. There were open fields only 10 meters farther on. Sometime later I heard as if from far away, as my father calling me. Jens, Jens can you hear me? I slowly regained consciousness and replied, yes. Then I noticed that my leg hurt. I screamed, my leg, my leg. I noticed that the pain was coming from my knee. I said it's my knee, my knee before losing consciousness again. Then something happened, that as a 13 year old boy, I could not understand. I found myself wrapped in blankets lying on the highway. I saw myself and other people very well and clearly. I felt no pain, and neither heat nor cold. I had the feeling of just being there and watching the action below.

I cannot say, how long it lasted, but I have never forgotten this experience. When I spoke later about that, nobody could understand it and said to me that I had probably only imagined it. I let it be, but knew that it was not my imagination. For me, it had been a different type of experience. I really did not understand at this time, but I started to think about it. So the time passed after this experience, and only my mother noticed how much I had changed since the accident. Once she said to me, "Since the accident, you are no longer the same". She was correct; this represented a deep experience in my life, and one that would lead me to "The Knowledge" through the years.

But there were still many hurdles to overcome. I noticed more and more clearly, that difficult situations in which I was sad and full of grief and sorrow, immediately impacted heavily on all areas of my life. This maelstrom of grief that I felt, took everything with it. How often I asked God, to take to him please, because I could not deal with these feelings. But he had other plans for me.

Again and again I fell and had to get up again, in all areas of my life. But I was always healthy and I was very grateful for this. It seemed that everything that I built up, I lost again. I asked myself, why this was so and what I can do to change it, but I did not recognize yet, what life was saying to me. I was still involved too much in my old patterns and the devastating emotional outcome. I remember after I had divorced, my business had ended, and I was at the end of my tether. My level of optimism was rock bottom. During this time I had a lot of contact with my sister, she had just been to see a healer and recommended me to try it also. I said, OK, why not, having nothing to lose. So I made an appointment, not having any idea of what awaited me there.

My first time with a healer...

I was greeted warmly and after a short conversation, he suggested that I should lie down and close my eyes. Immediately, I noticed that I had trouble controlling my breathing. For me, who wanted always to have everything under control, it was an unbelievable experience. My breath did what it wanted, I let it happen and at some point, it calmed down. This was the beginning of my spiritual opening, although I did not know it at that time. When I look back I can see now, how my own transformation began. How arrogance can be transformed into humility, disbelief in faith, anger and hatred in love. Slowly *"The Knowledge"* began to have its affect within me.

We have to learn trust

Had I known at this time the significance of this, I would certainly have taken a different route, because my own personal selfishness did not allow it. But it is both good and important to keep certain things hidden from even ourselves, so that we can learn to trust. I attended some more personal sessions with the healer, and I began to feel better and better. I could "breathe again emotionally". But there were tougher tests to come.

Above all, in the area of love

This struck me many times that it was too expensive," as I thought. Also here I should learn to understand these painful emotions in order to transform them. I should learn to love, without imposing conditions. Those who can love freely, and unconditionally, are free.

I had to learn to understand this first of all. I really thought I knew what love is. But I didn't ... and I needed a decisive experience.

Thus it happened some years ago and it hit me completely unprepared. At this time, I was not aware of these things and they did not have much meaning for me. Spirituality, Religion, God, Angels, the Universe with its rules and principles, these things to me had no meaning... really nothing ... Although I thought that there was something higher, I had created my own idea of these things. At this time I was not aware of many things, they did not have much meaning for me. Then again something happened few years ago... something that would change my perception.

I experienced love in a form that I had never felt before

At that time I was tired from work and at home, in the afternoon. I lay down on the sofa and rested a little. What happened then is not something that I can put simply in words, because it was a feeling that I had never known before and it was so unexpected. It seemed as if my consciousness suddenly was raised and so I was in a vibration of love that I had never experienced before. I was not a part of this love, 'I WAS' this love. I felt nothing else, no thought bothered me and it felt like an infinite being, which has only one expression, Love. No words and nobody can describe that feeling really.

One can only truly understand it if one has experienced it, and also afterwards, it cannot be truly explained, because it is something that can only be described in the experiencing of it. I recognized that the love I had known before in my life, is nothing, when compared to the love that I experienced at that moment. I had thought before, that in my life, I had the ability to be able to love and I now recognized, that this was not so. Thus every person believes and makes his own personal experience. Often we attach conditions to love and often we are in a mutual emotional dependence, with the person which we believe we love. Is this love?   Yes! It is one form of its expression.

The Knowledge will be able to lead you, around all of these entanglements, those that hinder and bind us down into old patterns. To find a way out of these stuck habits therefore, is to be able to create a new, healthy and solid basis for our internal freedom, a prosperity, a fullness, a mental strength, a calmness, a new health, good relationships etc.

How did 'The Knowledge' come to me?

"The Knowledge" came in different ways to me. In the beginning, it came through books, people, and teachers who came into my life, and also the events that I organized. More and more I realized that "Knowledge" comes from within; as an inner voice that I noticed more and more. I heard that inner voice for a long time. "The Knowledge" gradually came also by feelings, that I had suddenly, and mental images, which appeared to me. For a long time, I ignored what I was getting, preferring the type of knowledge that everyone knows, because I did not want to succumb to, what I thought was my own fantasy.

But, as I slowly developed more confidence in "The Knowledge"

I began to get more and more evidence in the form of images, words and feelings. Even specific names of people that I did not know. It happened during individual sessions with people and in other ways. I gradually realized that I, as the man that I am, with the name that was given to me, could not know all of these things.

The Knowledge – It is within each of us

Introduction

People are always looking for more happiness, satisfaction, joy and inner peace. As a source for this, there is the power of the Universal Mind, which may be revealed to us as knowledge and wisdom so that we can live in balanced and in a fulfilled way. Each of us can find a way to this universal and infinite knowledge. It is within us and is just waiting to be discovered. This energy glows and shines in our hearts, even if we do not perceive it. In the entire universe universal principles work and thus they act also in us.

Wise teachers of all epochs recognized these principles and knew how to apply them. They have an effect in every second of our life and appear in our thinking and feeling by which words we are allowed to choose and therefore our actions follow. Hermes Trismegistos said: „ As above so below, as below so above". Everything is connected with one another and it has therefore a direct influence on our life. There are no exceptions and that which happens in our life, we have created ourselves. Then we cannot act simply in such a way, as if it would suffice to wish something different in our life in order to change the circumstances in our life. We should recognize the precise reasons, why things are exactly in a certain way in our life, so that we can change it successfully. If we don't understand that how we would we are able to change it? However, everything is in us and starts with the feeling of peace in us.

"The Knowledge"opens all the doors for those who understand these principles and learn to apply them. It will start to work in it infinite wisdom, without exception, to support and to lead everyone in all areas of life.

In this book you will find the guidance for it, so that „The Knowledge " is revealed in your life. Thus we learn to focus our attention on what really supports us and helps us to further us in life. The exercises in this book are very helpful and I recommend you to apply it. Only you can shape your live, happily, fulfilled, satisfied with an amazing inner balance. The biggest and most exciting journey can be starting in your live.

A journey to your true self.

Chapter 1

The Knowledge about the 7 principles
of the universe

*"If we begin to recognize which principles act
within us, we can use them for our welfare
and the welfare of others"*

Jens Behrmann

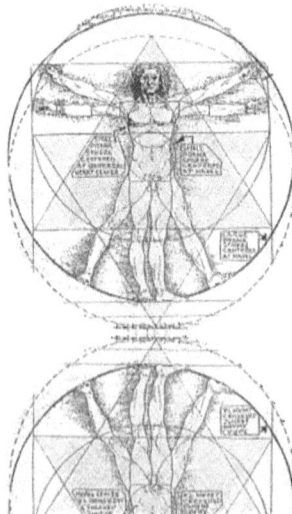

1. We live in a mental universe

In this universe there is the mind or if you wish, the spirit. Everything is imbued with this mind, and it is the bearer of all life. The mind exists in many different vibrations and is the full expression of wisdom, perfect love, and purity. Everything then that exists is either what we know or what we do not yet know. Everything that we touch, feel, see, smell and taste has been created from within this basic level of knowing. This then is the basic principle from within which, the whole creation exists. Also we use this mind within every second of our lives. Without it we could neither think nor feel, or move. Indeed, many of us are not aware of the fact, that we create the mind that we use in every second of our lives.

We think, see, feel and act. So we create in every second, living forms that can benefit us or harm us. We use our free will, and we can use it for everything good or for everything bad. It is up to us as to where we place our focus.

What does this mean exactly?

This means that somebody has the ability to concentrate extremely well and focus his thoughts in a disciplined way. If we can grasp this principle, and learn to apply it for ourselves, we can use it consciously to create substantial progress in all areas of our life. In order to do this, it is important first of all, that we are

motivated towards wanting change within our
thoughts, feelings, actions, this has got to be
recognized in order for real progress to be made.

Why we find ourselves in this or that situation,
what has brought us to this, how can I improve
the one or the other in my life, and what are the
prerequisites for this? How can we improve on
our 'luck' or 'good fortune' and reduce or
remove the things that hinder and bind us? If we
can learn more about the nature of the universe
that we are in, then we will be more and more
able to do this. The exercises in this book can
lead you to this knowledge.

2. Everything exists within two poles

Everything exists within two poles and we can arrange them from good to bad. Let us imagine, we have a thermometer; where does our sense of 'heat' begin and where does our sense of 'cold' begin? Whether water becomes steam or ice, it is still water. It differs only within the state of vibration or oscillation. Where does the light begin and where does darkness end? In the same fashion we can examine all aspects of our life like success, relationships, work, health, etc.

Where we choose to place ourselves on the scale of, very good to very bad: this is the same question in all of the different areas of our lives. This is what must bring into our awareness. Where does love begin, and where does the hatred begin? They are so different in their

expressions, but they arise from the same energy. We decide with our thoughts, feelings, words and actions, where and how we move on the scale. There are so many different expressions for all the properties that we develop in our lives and we can transform the ones that bother us. If you began to do that you will give "The Knowledge" more space in your life and it will begin to lead you to take more appropriate decisions.

3. As above so below, as below so above

This principle is extremely important for us because it shows us that everything has a counterpart at another level, and also that these levels influence each other all of the time. This applies to the material/physical level, on the emotional/psychic level, and the mental/spiritual level. If we are able to grasp this principle, we will be able to apply it within our own lives, and so many of the secrets that we still do not understand now, will be revealed. It is an ancient cosmic law upon which it is worthwhile to meditate. There is a duality of creation, and in every human being it is visible. It means for us that everything is already there. All is One.

If I would like to reach something in my own life and think about it, in this precise moment I have already reached it. At the spiritual/mental level it already exists, however, it is not visible for us yet at a material or physical level. This is the duality of creation since the unity is 'as above so below', and because we are spiritual beings, there is no difference. Everything is here already. As we begin to understand this principle, we will be able to remove many obstacles, and most of 'the veil of ignorance' will be lifted from us.

4. Everything is moving, and everything is vibration

Modern science confirms this statement, which the acient Egyptians knew to use quite early for themselves. However, over the course of time a lot has fallen into oblivion. We can see through studying this principle that all manifestations are based on the existence of different vibrations . Everything is Mind. This applies to the grossest matter back up, to the highest vibrations.

The pure mind is imbued with All-Wisdom, All-Power and Infinitive Love. We use this mind every second of our lives with our thinking and feeling, thus changing its vibration, depending on which higher or lower ideals we follow. One can say that we often abuse it unconsciously because we often use it for our own selfish purposes, and thereby we create a bad karmic effect. Do we understand this principle, we learn to control our own vibrations and so we learn to change them self-confidently, so that we generate an internal vibration which corresponds to our desire.

5. Male and Female

The dual principle is active in all that we know or don't know. The sun is the fire and the fire is male. From this fire there originates the light and the light is female. Thus the male and female principle reveals itself to us already, within the origin of the universe. In the man there is always a female part, and in the woman there is always a male part. We find this principle in the whole of creation. We must open only our eyes to see it. So we can find ourselves within an eternal creational process, within the creation of the Absolute Infinite Being. Everything in it is serving to expand and evolve, otherwise we would not develop. We use this principle in every second of our life.

Even if we are not aware of it: *We create perpetually.*

How we use it, depends on how clear one becomes of it, which in turn reflects upon how it has been used and understood in the past, leading up to the now. If we understand this principle properly, some doors will open.

6. The right Rhythm

We all know the rhythm of ebb and flow, the rhythm of the seasons, the pendulum of the clock, which swings from right to left. Everything moves and everything has its own timing. We also move and have our timeing. How many times do we have the feeling of having accomplished a lot, in order to determine the next moment, and then feel that nothing that we have done helped or even it may feel like a step backwards. We inhale and we exhale. Each of us has his rhythm and we all follow this rhythm of the entire universe, but sometimes we will not swing with this rhythm. Often we are not aware of this. Thus will create and destroy. If we look back in the history, we can see how whole nations have arisen, and then sunk down again. Let us learn to apply this principle for ourselves and use this principle by means of our self-control; so that we feel no more stuck and helpless in our lives. We start to swing with the rhythm.

7. Cause and Effect

All cause has its effect, and every effect is based on a cause. Coincidences do not exist. If we begin to understand that, then it is not important whether we are aware of it or not, we can discover herein a higher law, by which everything is over-ridden. The task is to discover it for ourselves, in that way, we can be raised to a higher spiritual plan. To be able to distinguish between efficient causes, and to learn what really is my own desire and my own will, and not the desire or the will of another man, which I may follow, as the will of another may be stronger than mine. Then we will recognize how we can think ahead and can estimate all consequences of our actions. We learn to master all circumstances in our life and are no longer dominated by them.

My Notes

Chapter 2

The Knowledge about Thoughts

"The happiness of your life depends
on the nature of your thoughts"

Marcus Aurelius - Roman Emperor

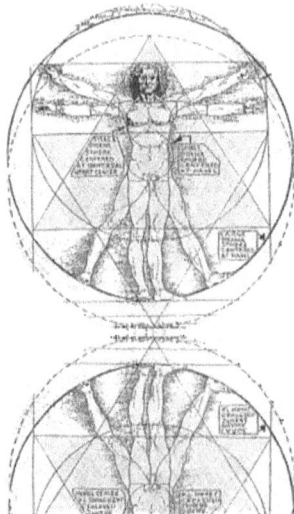

Scientists take the view that a thought is a firework of neuronal activity. Thoughts are caused by neurons, the brain's building blocks. A human being contains about one trillion of these nerve cells. They present information in the form of electrical impulses and pass them on at an incredible speed. A thought is faster than sound, faster than the speed of light, and light has a speed of 186411.3 mph. Our thoughts are already there before we are even aware of them. They shape themselves into information. This is the process that occurs in the brain and ultimately forms the thought, and this process continues unconsciously until it is completed. Then we become aware of the thought. The spiritual view is that a thought is built of etheric / aether energy* and it consists of light in different vibrations. Out of these different vibrations arises, for example, the entire spectrum of color in nature. All the emotional and mental feelings and experiences we are capable of originate from this energy of light.

It's like a living organism, which corresponds to the different light energy vibrations produced according to the emotional and mental states we create. In this way, different vibrations of light develop depending on what we think and feel. This etheric energy that is built by our thoughts is neutral in its nature, and we decide which vibrations of light we produce with every thought. The more loving, clear and positive our thoughts are, the more filled with light are the vibrations we produce.

*Etheric / Aether Energy is also known as Prana. This energy influence and corresponds with our bodies.

The more negative our thought, the darker is the light we produce and accordingly the vibration we send out. The world of emotions and the world of thoughts are connected in such a special way that it's important to learn to consider thoughts and emotions separately. There is hardly a thought without emotion and in each emotion there is always a part of a thought. Our thoughts and emotions form the essence of who and what we are. They shape our character and they make up our personality. Once an idea has been thought and sent out into the world, it will have an influence on our life. To which extent this happens, depends on the intensity of emotion and strength that we give to this thought. The more consciously we create a thought, the stronger is its mode of action or response. Etheric energy permeates the entire universe, and it permeates everything we know or do not know. It is a mental principle that works within the entire universe.

This is what is meant by: *"As above, so below and as below so above".*

In the chapter The Spirit / Mind I give closer consideration to this subject. Everything we encounter in the physical realm has its counterpart on the mental level, and vice versa. In this way, thoughts take shape and they always ensure that what we consciously or unconsciously send out, we will, sooner or later, receive. This may be something positive that constructively supports ourselves and others, or it may be negative and keep us stuck.

Every wrong thought can keep us stuck. Do we want to retain good or bad thoughts? Thoughts influence every second of our life. A person has about 60,000-70,000 thoughts per day. Who can tell which of those are conscious and which are unconscious? But all these thoughts influence our life. They affect our body, our success, our well-being and how we experience joy and sorrow. Let us ask ourselves: which thoughts are influencing our life? Are they thoughts of love, joy, beauty and harmony? Or are they mostly thoughts of jealousy, envy, hatred, or worse? Everyone knows the story of Aladdin and the Magic Lamp. Aladdin has three wishes, and it does not matter what these wishes are - they are fulfilled by the genie. It's the same with the thoughts we produce. However, we have not only three, but an infinite number of wishes. Are we clear about the quality of the ideas we have created within us and are sending out into the world around us?

Do we understand that our thoughts are reflected in the external circumstances of our life? We should pay close attention to what we think and what intentions we make visible through our thoughts and actions. Do they result in good positive action for ourselves and for others, or are the resulting actions less good? What impact do these actions have on us, and those around us? When we realize that everything that happens in our life is based on our own world of thought, we can perhaps accept that we alone are responsible for all the circumstances that arise in our life, and that we have brought them about, consciously or unconsciously. Then we have the opportunity to realize that we can consciously influence our life and point it into a direction that is good for ourselves and for others. We begin to comprehend what controls our life and how we end up in situations that are either good, bad or neutral for us. Then we can start to understand what makes up our personality and what constrains us. We can start to clean up our personality bit by bit by immediately changing destructive thoughts and emotions. We are constantly surrounded by countless and diverse information in the form of thoughts, which we continually takes in and reject again. Many people can feel this and sometimes it's as though we do not know exactly where this or that kind of thought is coming from. Sometimes there are thoughts that do not match our personality; these are thoughts we have taken on from other people.

This phenomenon is called clairsentience

We feel what the other thinks or feels. This shows us that thoughts are alive and independent; they make themselves known within their environment. People are both their transmitters and their receivers.

Imagine it like this:

Almost every one of us has played in a sandbox as a child. We had a small shovel, a rake, perhaps a broom for cleaning, and moulds for the sand. We would fill these moulds with sand and create a corresponding shape. It's the same with our thoughts. We constantly shape our thoughts on the mental plane and receive their counterparts in our physical world. They can manifest in physical or emotional form. Our actions are usually unconscious. Many people say, therefore, that we should be very aware of the way we deal with our thoughts. The more often we have a thought, the more powerful this thought becomes. It can start to dominate even our personality. Thus, we can develop phobias, addictions and all kinds of dependencies. Every thought, every feeling and every wish produces a thought form that we send out. In any way, it takes on its own existence. We differentiate between two types of thought forms. There are those that we can create by ourselves through a feeling or desire, and there are those that we give new energy to. The latter have been created before; they came into existence and discharged their energy. But their form continues and they can be recharged with energy, this happens when we send out a corresponding emotional vibration or a feeling that matches this thought form. However, we have the ability to generate two kinds of wish-fulfilling thoughts.

If negative emotions dominate a thought, then we create emotionally loaded thought forms, a kind of wishful thinking, which can often be destructive. But if we are guided by reason and love, we generate constructive ideas, thoughts in form of positive desires. Once a thought form of whatever kind exists, it can never be destroyed and will be re-energized until it has been fulfilled. We can however de-energize it. We do this by giving it no more attention, and eventually it will dissolve by itself and no longer affect us. That's because we no longer feed it with energy. This shows us that we have a choice: what do we want our life to be affected by?

That's what is meant by the saying: *"The spirits I've called..."*

Of course, this can also benefit us if we send out loving and positive thoughts. With each transmission, we are strengthening our positive personality and create a richer expression of ourselves, and therefore we should create thought forms that strongly support us, by beginning to think gentle, peaceful and constructive thoughts. Once we realize how powerful thoughts can be, we hold a key in our hand that we can use for our welfare and the welfare of others. Thoughts (Thought Forms) can help, support and heal, or they can destroy. Thoughts can cure or cause disease, and make people change their behavior. One could even say that they can cause phenomena. Each one of us is composed of his or her individual thoughts and they are extremely powerful. Every thought has an effect. Many tests have confirmed that our minds can override even the effects of drugs. Wounds heal faster, pain is reduced, and impaired motor skills can be improved.

We should consider the following:

All thoughts that we send out are indestructible and have a direct impact on our life. They are like a fingerprint that is unique to us. Thought forms have the intelligence of their creator and take on a form. That is why we call them thought forms. As creators of our thought forms, we are confronted with our creations. All this happens so that our imperfect forms of thought can be released. This can happen only through love and understanding. That's how we achieve perfection. Once that happens, our imperfect thought creations can be released. All of this can be achieved in conjunction with visualization. I shall discuss this in a later chapter.

Chapter 3

The Knowledge about Personality and Emotions

"The character is based on the personality, not on the talents."

Johann Wolfgang von Goethe

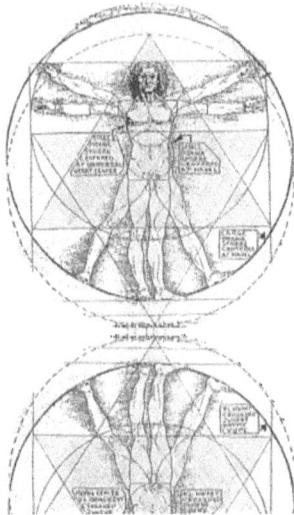

Our personality is in a constant state of flux. It may have wonderful and euphoric feelings today, but tomorrow it may feel entirely different. The personality and the feelings and actions that emanate from it are often dependent on external circumstances, whether they are to our advantage or not. If we have a positive experience, we are happy, if our experiences are less good, we are less happy or even unhappy. Where is the common denominator? Who or what causes pain, suffering and confusion? What causes conflict, violence, grief and even war? What is the reason for love, joy, happiness and peace? The Norwegian Academy of Sciences has estimated that over the past 3,600 years about 15.513 wars took place, resulting in 3.064 billion deaths.

Why does this happen?

It happens because our subconscious personality is responsible for everything that is good and bad in this world. So what constitutes our personality? We can say that the personality is the sum total of all experiences, emotions, thoughts and deeds in our life. No two personalities are the same. Even identical twins have two different personalities. Ultimately, the Personality is a part of the lower egoism. Selfishness will prevail and abuses the spirit for its own selfish lower emotions and desires. These include greed, envy and malice. This is the way so much evil is brought to the fore within us. Our real self, that part of our true being often suppressed by our selfishness, is reflected in a sensible and loving personality. So the personality's lower egoism tends to exist on the lowest level of consciousness and is responsible for all the suffering in this world. Recognizing that, we have the ability to extend our awareness of lower egoism and transform it into a loving expression of life. It must be dismantled so that our life will be filled with more joy, happiness, contentment, love, peace and all that we desire. In this way, we change our own vibrational resonance. We are always the ones who decide.

But how can we recognize our egoism?

We recognize it when we start to look very clearly at the circumstances of our life. This enables us to achieve some clarity about our motives and motivation for our aims, our current life and what has caused the circumstances we live in. If our motivation only serves our personal development at the expense of other people and if we have created in and therefore around, us a lower and egoistic climate, then we can be sure that we serve only our lower ego state. If we then start to observe ourselves, we have the opportunity to create change in ourselves, slowly and sustainably. We achieve this by practicing to be attentive. In that way, we can consciously begin to discover our real nature, the nature of our higher self.

Because we now focus on our loving nature, we become aware of our self in its wholeness and begin to discover our loving nature. Gradually, we grow in consciousness. By making use of the keys that are within us, we also make conscious use of the consciousness principle.

These keys are: *Meditation, observation, concentration, contemplation and introspection.* More about this later.

The lower selfishness of our personality can be a constant factor of uncertainty in our life. Bringing it under control is a difficult task and requires daily practice.

Let me give you an example:

Have you ever been unlucky in love? Practically everyone knows the sad feeling of being abandoned. Most of us have some experience of how our emotions can influence our thoughts, even our health, our appetite and many other things. Do you remember?

The question that arises here is:

Why is it so difficult to get out of this vicious cycle of emotions that are not good for us and influence the world of our thoughts?

The reason is that these emotions focus the attention on suffering. These lower emotions determine the thoughts while also continuing to produce vibrations. The thought forms are charged with more and more energy and we get more of what we do not really want: lovesickness. It's a chain reaction that feeds on itself and is reflected in a variety of life circumstances. Of course, this principle also applies to joy, happiness, contentment, and anything else in our life. Not without reason is it said that money always comes to those who have a lot of it already. Often more and more money comes easily to those who already have lots. It's the same principle, and it's not a coincidence. It is because of the thoughts they think habitually. The good news is that it does not matter in what social environment you grew up or how you live now. At any time, you have the ability to refocus your thoughts in a way that changes your circumstances, and so changes your whole life. We do this already, in every moment, but mostly we do this unconsciously. We need to become aware of this part of our being. The world and all we know, consists of thoughts. The speed with which they move is unimaginable for us. A thought is vibration and light, and once created, it cannot be eliminated. It can reach any part of the universe and corresponds with people who have similar vibrations, thus contributing to intensify good or bad.

Do we have good and noble intentions or are our motives selfish and full of hatred, envy, jealousy and revenge?

The way we think generates vibrations that reach every cell in our body. Selfishness is the sum total of our lower thought forms, and therefore the source of any disease in our personality, and is responsible for all the suffering in this world. Our true nature, our true self, gives out personal love, compassion and good deeds that result from good positive thinking and good emotions. We alone are responsible for the path we choose. Think of Dr. Jekyll and Mr. Hyde. It is a superb example and shows us very clearly the nature of lower selfishness and the ego that exists or can exist within a personality. When we begin with our destructive thoughts, we begin to destroy our cells and will eventually suffer physical disease. This then will cause our body to sicken and wither like a flower. But with every loving thought we think, our body comes into harmony and will blossom and shine like a beautiful flower.

Chapter 4

The Knowledge about
Spirit / Mind

*"The biggest decision of your life is that you can change
your life by changing your mindset."*

Albert Schweitzer

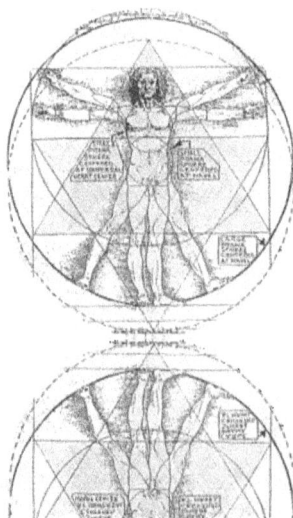

What do we mean when we talk about the mind? Thinking of the skills people usually connect with the mind, it is perception and learning as well as remembering and imagining and fantasizing and all forms of thinking. This includes planning, considering, selecting, making decisions evaluating, being mindful and much more. But, above all, a good state of mind also requires a high degree of concentration. The spiritual aspect of Mind or Spirit is something that is not tied to our physical body. Everything that lives, whether we know it or not, is imbued with spirit on different vibrational frequencies, which most people cannot perceive.

Mind springs from the divine consciousness, and is steeped in the omnipotence and All-Love and the All-Wisdom of the Creator. Mind is the substance of which the entire creation makes use, and it is the bearer and the expression of all life in a variety of vibrations. Our physical world is solidified mind, it is the lowest vibrational state of mind. In this state, the three-dimensional world and all the physical forms that we know are formed. Many religions include the idea of a Holy Spirit and in Christianity, blessings end with the phrase "In the name of the Father, the Son and the Holy Spirit". This is how the Absolute expresses a higher consciousness and this Holy Spirit is what we can experience as universal wisdom and healing. The Holy Spirit has a special role to play around the world and in many different cultures. Its element is fire. John the Baptist said that he would baptize with water, but that he was the forerunner of the one who would baptize with fire, Jesus the Christ. We all know the saying that someone who had to prove himself in a new environment has come through a baptism of fire. Everything has a meaning in our language, and often this meaning is derived from ancient customs and traditions.

But what does the mind enable us to do?

The mind is available to people in various vibrational frequencies and we can learn bit by bit to consciously make use of the mind. If we do well when we consciously use the mind, then we will be able to understand this mental principle better and achieve better results. I previously stated that the mind pervades everything, from the most subtle to all kinds of solid bodies and all manifestations, be they minerals, plants, animals or humans, throughout the entire universe and encompassing all we know and don't know. With our thoughts we shape the mind, and we all use the mind every day and every second of our life. Most people however do this unconsciously. The mind was made available to us as a tool to enable us to create in a conscious process of co-creation. Do we realize what a very great gift we have been provided with?

What means now as it stands in the Bible?

"Give us this day our daily bread."

This is meant to describe the etheric energy of a specific frequency that works in us. We receive this energy from the sun and we can absorb it very consciously during meditation, during breathing practice or even with the food we eat. If we always keep ourselves well filled up with etheric energy, we will feel better and healthier and we will more and more experience the spiritual side of ourselves. This spiritual awareness lies dormant within all of us and it permeates everyone. But as we do not consciously know about this, we attach no importance to it whatsoever. This is how many of us waste an incredible source of potential energy. I will give a simple example of how the spirit works within us. If you have managed to cope well with the sudden onset of a tricky situation, you would say that you have acted with presence of mind. The mind has become active in us, without us having had to consider it. In Latin, the word spiritus can mean either breath or mind, thereby making it obvious that we receive the spirit by breathing it into us. We take it in with our first breath and with our last breath it will be leaving our body.

We raise our awareness with various breathing exercises. For example, if we breathe consciously and deeply instead of drawing unconscious, shallow breaths, we will absorb more ethereal energy to strengthened us and make us feel full of vitality. True masters are able to save so much etheric energy through their controlled breathing, that they can pass it onto others without losing any of their own power. Good healers are also able to do this. Jesus Christ also gave out this etheric energy. He performed what we call miracles, but in reality they were things that correspond to our nature.

Jesus the Christ said, not without reason: "Truly, truly, I say to you, whoever believes in me will also do the works that I do; and greater works than these will he do, because I am going to the Father."

To achieve this, we must become clear about ourselves and clarify and clean up our personalities. This can be a lengthy process. But we have the opportunity to create with and through the mental principle. As I already mentioned above, we have the ability to shape the mind.

Therefore, the central question that arises here is:

To what end do I use the mind, and simultan-eously the etheric energy, at this moment, and what have I created so far and want to create now?

God in His infinite love, wisdom and goodness will provide each of us with everlasting etheric energy, given to us just like the daily bread from the Bible. If we consume it, because we are angry or carry hatred within us, we will get exhausted very quickly. Excitement and conflict always take up more space. It costs us more and more energy and finally we feel drained and tired, because we have expended a lot of energy on our anger. What would have happened if we had remained calm instead of fighting with each other, and we had invested no energy in this dispute? If we use the mind substance well and carry love and joy within us, then my supply of etheric vitality doesn't get used up so quickly. If we use it badly, our supply of etheric energy will dwindle much faster.

So we should learn to economize and avoid situations that cannot be good for us.

Now we know how the mind works, but how can we use it consciously?

We have the ability to utilize the conscious mind with our thoughts and thus we give it a shape. Every thought and every emotion creates a shape that comes back to us and affects our life. With just this information, each of us can begin to observe the process of how to integrate this knowledge into his own life and create thought forms that support the process of giving our life the direction we want it to take. The mind substance is the God-given resource for the purpose of fulfilling our desires. It does not matter whether we realize it or not. Whether we are conscious of it or not, this is what we do already. We should not use the mind to influence other people, but we should create thoughts of love and purity, peace, joy and beauty, of happiness for ourselves and for others. We live in a just system in which everything is exactly in its place. This happens by the thoughts we send out, and the quality of the vibration that we cause.

Everything in our life corresponds to and shows exactly what is our consistent vibration, because vibration cannot pretend like a human being can. Vibration extends with all the thoughts and emotions that we have created. We are always just there and we always learn and receive exactly what corresponds to these vibrations. We reap what we sow. So what do we need in order to achieve conscious change? We should learn to visualize. This universe, the entire cosmos and everything that exists is subject to the same mental principle. The mind is divine in its origin and its expression is therefore sacred. We should begin to think about why that is so, and how this principle and our knowing of this principle can constructively be applied to ourselves and to others. Thus we can start to transform destructive thought forms, which we can see in many destructive emotions and life circumstances, into something constructive and positive.

My Notes

Chapter 5

The Knowledge about Visualization

*"What you can see with the spirit,
you will receive."*

Jens Behrmann

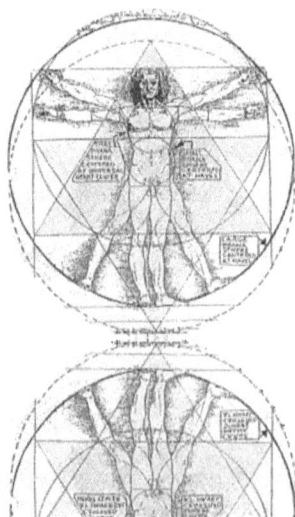

When visualizing, the mind is utilized with confidence to create brilliant and crystal clear detailed images. Looking at it this way, visualizing is the language of the divine within us. By learning and consciously using this divine language, we can change our entire life. Visualization can be applied to all areas of our life.

There is only one important rule that we should always and under any circumstances be aware of:

We should never use the visualization process to influence other people. We should never selfishly enforce that which does not respect the free will of a person.

This would eventually have unpleasant and probably also karmic consequences for us. If you want to practice diligently and learn to use to shape the spiritual substance of visualization, the best way to start is with simple images. Bit by bit we then start to generate entire settings and events. There is probably nothing more powerful than thoughts, and if we combine these confidently with visualization, then we gradually unfold our true self, and can also help others. Each of us subconsciously visualizes in our dreams and even in our waking state. Every one of us unconsciously has so-called daydreams in which we forget everything around us.

This exercise will help you understand:

Close your eyes and breathe rhythmically through the nose into the stomach and out through your mouth. You should breathe in for four seconds and exhale for four seconds. Once you are a little calmer, imagine, in great detail, a lemon. See the whole lemon, in every little detail, in your mind's eye, see the bright yellow color, the shape. Once you have this image, you can smell the lemon. What does it smell like? Perhaps you feel your mouth tightening, maybe it is watering? Now imagine that you cut the lemon in half. Look at the pulp very carefully and see how juicy it is. See the juice running down both halves of the lemon. Maybe you can smell the citric acid and can even taste it. After a while, put the two halves back together and see that the lemon is whole again. It's that easy to visualize, it is so easy to mold the mind and to communicate in a divine language.

Visualizing is the deliberate acting in spirit, and after much practice it is the deliberate creation of internal imagery with the mind. We can experience taste, feelings, colors and actions produced with inner images. This is a gift that each person carries within himself. We often unconsciously visualize, frequently only in our dreams. But even here we create realities that may be entirely real. On television, we tend to visualize what we are presented with.

A desire is awakened in us, because we have made a link to a stored emotional picture. Therefore, we should carefully examine whether something belongs to us, or whether it is something that awakened our emotions from the outside. Visualization is a divine language, the 'key' to the kingdoms of heaven. When we learn to observe carefully and to concentrate fully, we more and more gain the ability to visualize consciously.

We shape the energy to consciously create thought forms that serve us in a constructive way.

Chapter 6

The Knowledge about Inner Peace

*"If you cannot find your peace within yourself,
it is useless to seek it elsewhere."*

Francois de La Rochefoucauld

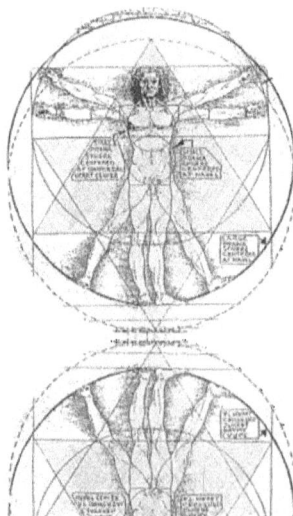

Inner peace is very important for us. Without inner peace, we cannot perceive our actual needs. If we have inner peace and quietude, we can generate great ideas, because we will be able to take advantage of our intuition. We find our center during periods of quiet and begin to regain a feeling of our true self. In times of quiet, ideas and views come to us that we cannot perceive in a hectic environment. It is enough to take a few minutes every day to grow quiet and really feel our inner peace.

In this time of inner peace we will see our own needs more clearly and will become more and more relaxed. The calmer and more relaxed we are, the stronger we will be able to exercise our intuition or inner voice. Many of us also call this our gut feeling. When we are at rest, we rediscover our true selves and we become open to our inner wisdom. Within us there is so much more knowledge than we can imagine at this point in time. How much rest do we allow ourselves every day? Do we truly allow ourselves to rest without external disturbances such as music, television or anything else that distracts and disrupts our time of rest? It is said that strength lies in calmness. Let us think about this phrase and its meaning for us. It is especially important at the beginning that we are patient with ourselves. Often, lots of thoughts intrude and distract us from our goal of attaining quietude. We should not let that discourage us and just carry on. The more we go into periods of quiet, the more peaceful our thoughts will become and we will make real progress every day. Even if in the beginning we find only a few seconds of inner peace, we will then be able to extend this period by a few more seconds. We should practice and not be discouraged by setbacks. That way, we will get better and better in time. Eventually, our thoughts will always be quiet, as we continue to learn to control our thoughts. The magic word for finding our inner peace and quietude is: *Patience.*

My Notes

Chapter 7

The Knowledge about Silence

"The silence knows all secrets."

Jens Behrmann

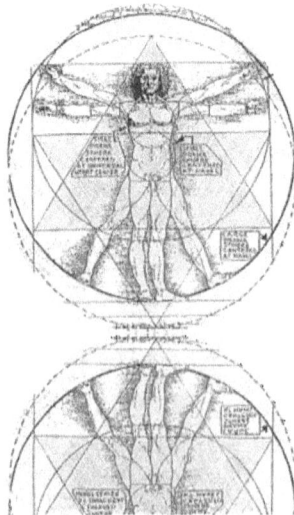

The word silence means absence of movement and absence of sound. Finding your own silence therefore means the absence of noise of any kind on the outside and especially inside of us. We aren't distracted by anything. The busy-ness of daily life, which surrounds us more or less every day, causes us to focus predominantly on that which is outside of us. Out shopping or at the train station, we mostly concentrate on just trying to get from A to B without collision. In addition, we are practically bombarded with all kinds of information such as advertising, a cacophony of voices, announcements, music, cell phones ringing, etc.

We absorb information from all that surrounds us, and we process it constantly. It is enough to make us feel inwardly restless and tense even hours later. The difference between quietude and silence is that while we may have quietude around us, it does not necessarily mean that we carry silence within ourselves. Quietude is the absence of noise, and silence is what we carry within ourselves. Silence is a great luxury that we do not allow ourselves enough of these days. Instead, we go to great lengths to find relaxation. We visit the sauna, have a massage, have spa weekends, go running to keep fit, etc. But even then, we remain in most cases in the outside world and not in our inner world. Many wise teachers speak of silence and that we should utilize it every day.

Why?

In silence we can become aware of the desires, words and deeds that are within us. In silence we can become aware of and recognize the emotions and thoughts that are within us. We should listen carefully to our inner voice and recognize what is not in harmony within us. Silence can make many things recognizable for us and when we become aware of our destructive thoughts and emotions, we can change them. But above all, silence enables us to access another level of our being. When we are in silence and close our eyes, we leave the physical plane and enter the psychic plane. We enter our inner world. Here, our perception of the world within us and around us is completely different. Both worlds exist side by side and simultaneously. But we often perceive our inner world only when we are in silence.

My Notes

Chapter 8

The Knowledge about Love
and the Human Being

"In the beginning all thoughts are of love.
Later all love belongs to the thoughts."

Albert Einstein

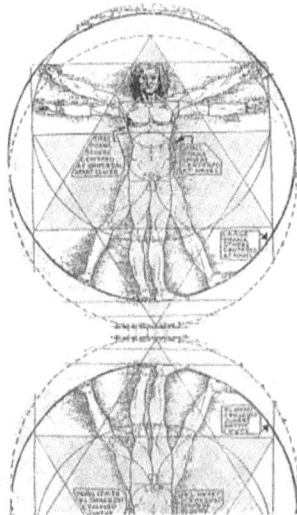

Love has always been one of the most popular themes in literature, songs and conversation. After all, love is the most important thing in the universe. Everything is created by love, everything is maintained by love and everything shall be transformed by love. If we meet every person with love, regardless of who he is, what he says and what he does, we are on the right track. Many outstanding personalities who have made great contributions to mankind advise us to follow this path. I had an experience of love that has changed my way of looking at love, and my feelings of love, forever. I was home from work one afternoon and decided to take a little break.

So I lay down on my bed, made myself comfortable and idly let my thoughts drift by. What happened next is not easy to put into words. I suddenly had the feeling that my consciousness was expanding. I experienced a completely new way of being. I found myself on a level where there were no questions. All was perfect. Personality did not matter anymore and I was infused with a feeling that enabled me to understand everything. At that moment I realized that everything is filled with great and infinite love. I've never felt love like that before; it is incomparable. In this feeling of absolute love, there is no hate, no envy, no jealousy or other destructive emotions. There are no thoughts, but everything seems to be only one loving thought. Everything just is, and I began to understand that everything is pure love on this level. At least that is the nearest word we have for this feeling. I understood that all the negative qualities exist only in my thoughts and feelings. But at the same time, there is this other reality on this other level. On this level within us, there is only this state of Absolute Love in which we exist and always will exist. To be able to feel this, we need to change our vibration to another level within ourselves. To feel this love was one of the greatest and most wonderful moments of this life for me. It is not possible to adequately describe this with words. To get there, it is absolutely necessary that we transform any destructive feelings and thoughts within us with love, and so release them. Then our feelings and our thoughts will be free from egotistical longings and limitations and our life will achieve a whole new meaning. If we pursue this course, then we will eventually be able to become a shining example of humanity, for ourselves and for other people. There have been those who have developed this very important attribute.

Let us consider just three public figures: *Gandhi, Mother Teresa or Nelson Mandela.*

They had such love that they served others selflessly and were able to give hope and encourage others, even an entire continent. They achieved great things under most difficult circumstances. This may not be our goal, but if we start on our way by bringing more love and self-love into our life, we will be able to change a lot for ourselves and also for other people. Love and joy provide the energy we need for everything we do in our life. They should be the foundation on which everything is based. If we sow love and joy, we shall reap more love and joy.

This is not always easy, but it is important to realize that we will already have achieved a great deal, if we become able to meet everything that happens in our life with love and joy. We will then take different decisions and begin to conduct ourselves differently; in particular we will start to clean up our personality and its inherent selfishness. We create a more loving version of ourselves. Our character will change and we will receive more self-confidence, greater self-esteem, greater joy, more serenity and inner peace. Many people are very stubborn and selfish. This also affects their approach to love. In relationships with other people, we place our love on the lowest level of experience. That is selfish love, where human beings only love themselves and are always concerned with their own advantage. Almost anything selfish we seek to achieve with other people originates from true and selfless love, but in the end only serves to make us feel good. Love should never be an end in itself and we should question our motives and feelings.

"Love is the secret to a successful life"

As we recognize that there no greater force in the universe than the love that is there, so, we begin to change our lives completely. With our muscles we can build or destroy, even destroy life. But the power of love, can open our heart and our soul. We can only meet the experience of life if we are immersed within love's art.

Many people like us, meet and greet with suspicion, they may have differing opinions than us, and perhaps they do not like our clothes or our character.

But, with love in us - this invisible force – it will reach and soften their hearts. As love enters you, it is as the sun melting ice, our love melting their heart. How can we achieve this love? Simple, we begin to love, within our lives and in all that we encounter. Love is present, to know, and to feel.

How can we achieve this love?

Let us begin to recognize the love that is present in our lives and that which is present in everything we encounter and feel. Especially the love that is present in that which we do not like. We make our way through life and slowly it frees us from the fears and anxieties that torture us. To be clear about these fears and anxieties, is to be free from them, it frees us from our inner constraints. Let us begin to recognize and to feel the love that is in our life and in everything that happens to us, especially in that which we do not like.

If we take this big step, we will begin to see many things in a different "light". Everything in our life can become easier in this way. It is our choice that we can make. The next chapters show you how it works.

My Notice

Chapter 9

The Knowledge about Forgiveness

*"The weak can never forgive.
Forgiveness is the attribute of the strong."*

Mahatma Gandhi

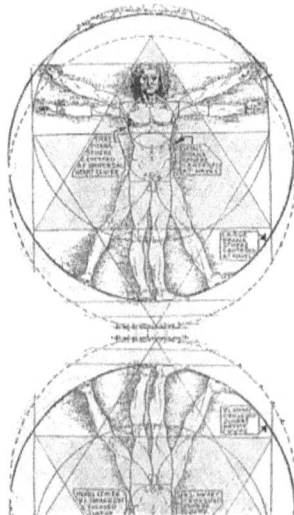

Forgiveness is one of the key aspects for us, and in Christianity and most other religions it is the central aspect. Jesus Christ said: "If I forgive, I forget." Forgiveness is the liberation from what binds us to something or someone in a destruct-tive way. Mostly this will concern experiences with other people. Forgiveness is not easy. How often do we find ourselves unable to forgive, or bad-mouthing someone, or harboring bad thoughts about someone who is not kindly disposed towards us or may even have harmed us? Every time we talk about these people, we do so in negative terms.

Considering the fact that everything is always in resonance with ourselves, we should investigate this behavior accurately. There must be something in our thoughts and feelings that corresponds exactly to that which we have experienced. There are no coincidences. Every cell in our body vibrates. This vibration corresponds to our thinking, feeling and acting. What we experience is what we have co-created ourselves. This is called resonance. We should stop blaming others for our personal failings, and begin to seek the causes of those failures in ourselves, so that we can forgive ourselves and others. If we do not, we are confronted with this type of vibration (which is within us) and will always have similar experiences. In addition, we bind thoughts of revenge or hatred to ourselves and so influence the character of our personality, where it remains and always wants to be supplied with energy. This zaps our strength and brings disquiet. How much grief and sorrow have been caused by the inability to forgive!

Entire wars have been started because of it and are still being started. A person should always be able to forgive himself and his neighbor with love.

If he can't, he will always look to blame others for his bad experiences and his failings. This is no way to find inner peace. Only when we accept our life circumstances independent of other people, we will be free and are able to discover that only we alone are responsible for everything good and bad in our life. Now we can live a life that we can build freely from our own selves. Very important, and this should apply not only to Christians, is that Jesus prayed on the cross for forgiveness for his enemies.

According to scripture, he said: "Father forgive them for they do not know what they are doing." Luke, 23, 24

This would make a very good guiding principle for us. Perhaps we can call this sentence to mind when we find ourselves in a situation where we have to deal with an unpleasant person. The Lord's Prayer also includes the request for forgiveness. Because of these historical facts alone, we can imagine what significance forgiveness could have for us. How many people cannot forgive and instead turn their thoughts to revenge only. An eye for eye, a tooth for a tooth has nothing to do with forgiveness. We would just create more conflict and impede our karma. There are people who bring untold suffering onto others, be it to get control over resources, or simply to do harm to other people, companies or even entire countries. All over the world, torture, murder and many unspeakable, evil acts of violence are committed against all kinds of living beings, be they humans, animals, plants or minerals. Why? Often, it involves control over people, even in our own relationships, and on other levels it may involve the control of resources so that someone or a company or a state has an advantage. Is this idea not incredibly petty and selfish? Maybe there is a better way for us. Looking at all this in relation to a person, we need to ask ourselves whether we want justice or just satisfaction, and what is it that we want to achieve with our actions?

Every person who retaliates for revenge, acts against the teachings of love and therefore against God. We then create our own fate, which is likely to be hard and certainly will not be kind to us. If we do not want this and forgo revenge, we create for ourselves a world that is always loving and kind towards us. That is because then we are able to be more at peace with ourselves. This is how we free ourselves from the cycle of cause and effect, and this is how we should deal with all the situations and circumstances in our life. I admit that the way of forgiveness is not an easy path, but it is so much shorter than the path of revenge and it leads us to a life of greater happiness and less suffering. To achieve this, we undoubtedly need to believe that, whatever circumstances we find ourselves in, we can change them again.

Chapter 10

The Knowledge about Faith

"Now faith is confidence in what we hope for and assurance about what we do not see."

(Hebrews 11:1)

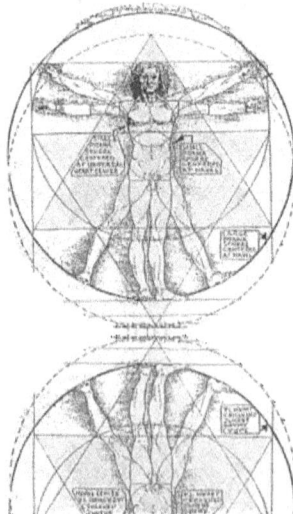

According to this quotation from the Bible, true faith is the result of spiritual development and self-realization. The five senses of the human body - sight, taste, hearing, smell and touch - are created for the perception of our surroundings, while faith does not question that which is hidden from these senses. Many people believe only that for which they can find material or physical proof. Many people associate a sensory experience with their faith. They do not believe something until they see it, and sometimes not even then.

It can also be the other way around:

Despite a strong belief in something you may find no evidence of it whatsoever in the material world.

Why is that? And what about those things we believe in?

Sometimes we have to recognize that we delude ourselves and that it is not yet the right time for the fulfillment of our desire. We should closely look at that which we hope for, and try to understand why it has not yet been fulfilled and even why we desire it at all. Perhaps an important realization is still missing and we still have to gain understanding about a number of issues in our life. Above all, we should be willing to allow change in our life. We should be prepared and consider the circumstances of our life, with clarity and self-responsibility. We should be clear in our minds that we alone are responsible for our life and the resulting life circumstances, which we believe in.

Once this is clear to us and we can accept it, we will be able to begin to take responsibility for ourselves and for our life. We can only receive things we wish to have when we are ready and when we believe. Everything that happens in life corresponds to our faith, because we live in a system of cause and effect.

What is really behind that which you wish and long for?

The Bible says in its Letter to James: "Faith without work is dead."

Many of us tend to have faith in an idea or a feeling and yet we take no action. We believe for only a tiny moment in ourselves and in our idea. Then we discard it all again. Faith will grow in us little by little and become a solid foundation only when we begin to act. Only then can we achieve a result. It should be self-evident to the reader that we should pursue only good purposes and should not abuse other people for our own selfish goals. If our faith is great enough, it becomes visible in the work that originates from it. If we are inactive we should ask ourselves why.

We should ask ourselves in what we believe. The ideas that we believe in need not always be big and impressive. They can be simple everyday things like cooking a good meal or taking a walk. There are many expressions of faith, either positive or negative. Everything seems to be ultimately a matter of the right faith, which then flows into good intentions. Faith works in various directions. I can create good things or the opposite.

82

And so the question for each of us is: What have I created in my life so far?

It does not matter whether this was done consciously or unconsciously. The belief in something is equivalent to a vibration that is sent out by us, consciously or unconsciously, and that will impact on us.

Chapter 11

The Knowledge about Word and Sound

"A word once uttered can never be recalled."

Horace

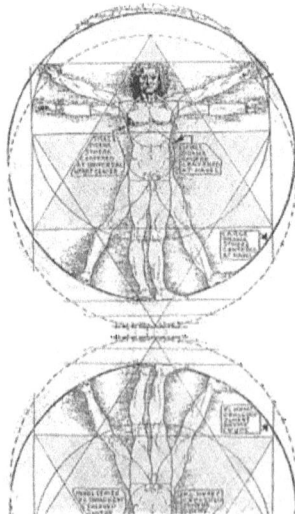

The Gospel according to John begins as follows:

"In the beginning was the Word and the Word was with God and the Word was God. Everything was created through the word, and without it nothing would come into existence. The word was life and this life was the light for all people. The light shines in the darkness but the darkness has closed itself to the light".

Words are given a position of outstanding importance in the scriptures of many religions. Words are an expression of our thoughts and emotions. In this sense they are a big part of our personality. Words are ultimately only a means of communication with other people. Almost all people have forgotten that we can communicate on other levels. When we enter a room where other people are arguing, then this vibration is noticeable in the air around us. At this level of feeling and adjusting to other people we can learn, even without words, what they feel or what vibrations surround us. But let us go back to the word. When we think and speak words, we build audible thought forms. They are living forms that we send out, just through our thoughts.

When we use good, benevolent and therefore constructive thoughts and words, good and benevolent encounters will come to us. When our words are more destructive, our experiences are also likely to be destructive at some point. The words we speak will sooner or later have an impact on our life. The spoken word reinforces what we think and feel. If we imagine that every thought is converted into a word we can hear, and everything we hear around us causes our cells to vibrate, then we should think very carefully about what influences we expose ourselves to. What kind of music do we listen to, what movies do we watch and what environment do we stay in?

Everything we experience as sound has a vibration and that vibration is again divided into light in many different colors. There are people who see musical notes as colors and can even taste them. This is called synesthesia. Their different way of perception gives us a glimpse of a possibility to experience the world in ways we all have within us, albeit mostly unconsciously. Synesthesia does exist in all of us, but we are not yet able to realize it, because we have not yet developed this concept within us. A word is sound, a sound is vibration and a vibration has a color. We often speak of tone color. Words we choose and how we express them have a corresponding effect. Whether we are conscious of this or not, it does not matter.

What about music?

Let's look at those who are fans of different styles of music. Classical music expresses itself differently to, for example, pop music. Pop is different to rock, which is unlike punk. Any music has its own sound and every singer has a different tone color. Each of us has an absolute preference for a certain style of music. We can say that we feel comfortable when something matches our vibration. If we don't like some style of music, we would hardly purchase a CD of it or listen to it on the radio. What sound does our voice have? How do we express ourselves? Do we speak loving and benevolent words? Each of us represents a particular vibrational frequency. A word or a sound reaches each one of some ten trillion cells in the human body and these vibrate. Even the words we choose and speak can reveal much about the circumstances in which we live. We should try to express ourselves more lovingly and justly. This is a good way to attract such treatment to ourselves. If we need to criticize others, we always have a choice of options open to us: we can express ourselves either in a loving or a hurtful manner. A word and a sound can open or close our hearts and the hearts of the many people we meet every day. It is our choice how we treat other humans or animals or all other living things. This choice is ours to make, and we make that choice during every second of our life.

What choice will you make for your life?

Chapter 12

The Knowledge about Prayer

"Prayer is the breath of the soul."

Johann Wolfgang von Goethe

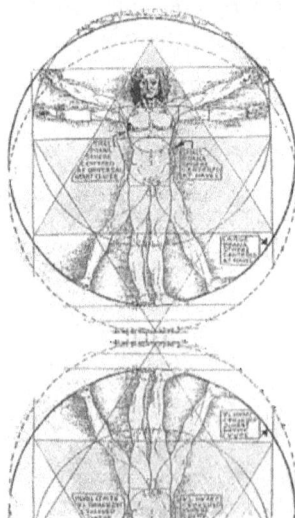

Regardless of what religion they belong to, people pray in all the countries around the globe. This shows how important prayer is in all the cultures and religions of the world.

Why is that?

Through prayer, we hope that our request will be heard and that whatever we desire will be given to us by God, Jesus, the Holy Spirit, Mother Mary, or by whomever this prayer is addressed to. We ask for help and support. Everybody wants to achieve a specific goal through their prayer and has this very clearly in mind. Through prayer, we create thought forms that correspond to a very clear purpose, and we fill them with energy by putting all our concentration into the prayer, so that it will serve its purpose.

Therefore, when we pray, we create a form from our thoughts and words. The content corresponds to our request and transmits the vibration that we created when we prayed. Most people do this very often, however unconsciously, because they have no idea what praying in its original form means. If we have previously expanded our consciousness and focused all our attention on the prayer, then we have reached a different vibrational frequency. At this frequency, we can generate thought forms that are more loving and more powerful than just a fleeting emotion, or a quick thought. If we then pray in accordance with the will of God, this prayer will be able to break through all boundaries. Prayer is a powerful key to our progress and the success of whatever projects we have planned. It does not matter what area of our life we want to progress. A prayer should always come from the heart. In our heart, we find the interface of our material and spiritual worlds.

A prayer from the heart always has a very good response and is very powerful. It is important to focus on the heart centre. Later, we'll learn an exercise for doing this. The Heart Math Institute in the U.S. has found that the vibration in our heart is 5,000 times higher than in other areas of our body such as the brain. If we focus on this, we have the ability to center ourselves, so that we can be pure and clear in our thoughts. We can then begin to pray more effectively and more powerfully. Of course, we can say a prayer out loud, quietly or even in our thoughts. That's not so important. Important for achieving our goals and desires is the vibration and resonance that we create when we pray from the heart. Below you'll find a prayer. Many people searching for the truth say this prayer every day. It is a match for a different state of mind that is extremely important for praying.

In Matthew 6.5-7 is the following statement

And when you pray, you shall not be like the hypocrites. For they love to pray standing in the synagogues and on the corners of the streets, that they may be seen by men. Assuredly, I say to you, they have their reward. But you, when you pray, go into your room, and when you have shut your door, pray to your Father who *is* in the secret *place;* and your Father who sees in secret will reward you openly. And when you pray, do not use vain repetitions as the heathen do. For they think that they will be heard for their many words. We should always pray with all our heart and with all our love. Then our prayer becomes a prayer of the heart. The Lord's Prayer has been somewhat modified here.

Before you begin to pray, focus on yourself a couple of minutes. If you like, you can make the basic meditation. You'll find this meditation in the exercise chapters of the book.

You can say this prayer, or any other prayer of our choice.

Our Father in heaven,

Hallowed be your name,

Your kingdom come,

Your will be done, on earth as in heaven.

Give us today our daily bread.

Forgive us our sins as we forgive our debtors

And lead us in temptation

And deliver us from evil.

For yours is the kingdom and the power and the glory forever. Amen.

It's enough to say a short prayer from the heart to get in contact with God, or Jesus the Christ or the Holy Spirit. This three are one.

My Notes

Chapter 13

The Knowledge about the interaction of the Will, the Intellect and the Heart.

„The power of thought, the power of will, the power of the heart belong to a perfect man"

Ludwig Feuerbach

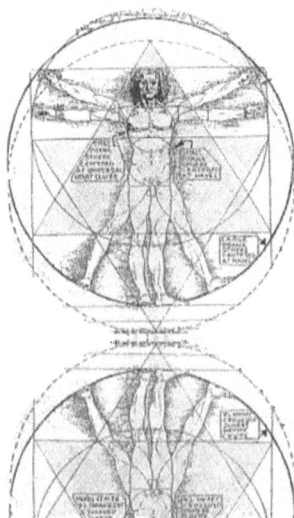

The will is purely spiritual and with it we can realize our goals. Do we want to implement our will? It is important then that we will develop good concentration, observational skills and staying power. Related to the will, is the ability to deal adequately with obstacles, which we are bound to meet on the way to reaching our goal. In that moment we need not let ourselves be discouraged. In this way we are able to reach our goal still determined. The measure in which we believe in the strength of our will and our own ability to achieve goals, also has to do with our levels of self-confidence.

The more confidence we can develop, the greater becomes the belief in ourselves, and thus an increase in our willpower.

How do we create will power?

As we think we both create and feel different vibrations. These vibrations are exactly a composition of the spirit / mind, which we use. We will call this our ability to 'Reason'. Next, if we examine 'will power' we will see that neither the 'clarity of our intellect', nor the 'strength of our heart' is included. These are all areas that make up 'willpower'. Reason / intellect - clarity and the connection to our heart.

Together, they all add up to our will, and then, depending on how well I can focus on myself, and what areas predominate, thus we generate the quality and strength of the will power, itself.

With the intellect, we focus on one thing, it is like a direct beam. With the heart, we create circular waves that spread in all directions and the will power then vibrate from top to bottom and from right to left.

Depending on how strong your will power is, you then generate this in a real way, setting these properties evenly.

How do you strengthen your willpower and how far are you willing to go? Is there a way to know that? Yes, of course, you can figure it out.

Two easy ways to finding out how strong your will is, are the following:

1. Using the time during which you usually get up to change. Let's say that you usually rise at 7:00 clock in the morning. Try changing the time that you rise to 6:00 clock in the morning. Doing this of course, without an alarm clock. From this simple example, we can learn how strong our will is. You should train your will until you succeed in getting up at 6:00 clock.

2. Test yourself to see if you fall asleep within 5 - 10 minutes. Have the intention that you will fall asleep during this time.

How strong is your will and how can you strengthen your will?

The first step:

First off all, you should be clear about what you actually want. Goals and desires can change quickly. Basically, everyone has a couple of basic goals in life from which it life deviates only reluctantly, and to which we, though perhaps unconsciously, work out. What are your goals? How should they affect you? Why do you want to achieve a specific goal and what are your motives?

These are fundamental questions on which you should be perfectly clear.

The second step:

You should begin to strengthen your self-confidence. Begin to think about your strengths and begin to emphasize your strengths. Begin to live more and more from these strengths. In this way, good properties will increase. Poor qualities will diminish. Autosuggestion is a good tool to change destructive and unconscious beliefs.

"Will power will bring success in all areas of your life."

Will power brings you the success you want in all areas of your life. We must not forget that we expend just as

97

much energy for the not so good circumstances in our lives as we do for the good circumstances, it takes the same Will Power. We need to see that what we actually achieve in these cases probably often unconsciously harms our life more than it benefits us, and only serves to keep us stuck. What good is it to have a lot of money if you cannot handle it, and then lead a life of debauchery through which you lose yourself? What good is the perfect love, if there is so much distrust and jealousy that it drives you crazy and if your loved one even dares to look at another one and you don't give yourself and others the space, because you are sick with jealousy? This all just brings dispute, grief and sorrow, and with it, many bad feelings for yourself and others. You should learn first of all, to recognize the destructive thoughts, emotions and behaviors in themselves, in order to transform them. He who wants to change something in his life should be in a position to correct the thoughts, emotions, motives and actions, with his Will Power.

Only then can he can overcome these obstacles.

These include primarily the destructive thoughts and emotions that hinder us and also bind us, because they generate a corresponding destructive vibration. The positive thoughts and emotions that we have, of course we should promote and strengthen. We are capable of doing this; we can then reach our targets despite adverse conditions, because the destructive no longer has power over us. He who has trained his willpower to be strong and good, achieves the goals more quickly and will overcome all the obstacles along the way.

My Notes

Chapter 14

The Knowledge about Introspection

"Whatever happiness we are looking for on the outside, we'll only be able to find within our inner being."

Jens Behrman

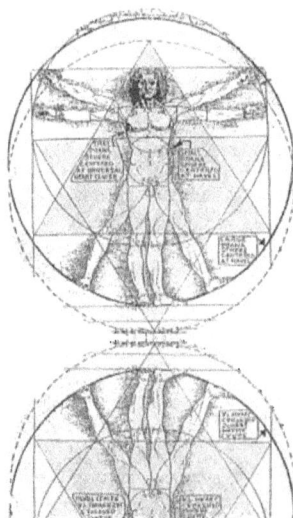

The purpose of introspection is to explore our inner selves. Here we can find the origins of our thoughts or emotions and the resulting behavior. Since our behavior exists on both the mental and the emotional level, introspection is about tracking down destructive thoughts or emotions and behavior in order to replace them with those that are loving and constructive. In introspection, a spiritual purification is taking place. This spiritual purification is something we should do for ourselves every day, just like we clean our physical body every day.

Everything that controls us mentally and emotionally in our being limits and dominates our life. In any case, it makes itself known by lack in many areas of life. Now we might think that lack may also be considered a form of wealth. Yes, that's true, but that kind of wealth is in its destructive form - whether it is expressed by sickness, financial problems, poor relationships or whatever else. Constructive abundance expresses itself always positively, i.e., in health, financial freedom, good relationships and much more. Introspection gives us the opportunity to free ourselves from all thoughts and emotions that we are burdened with. When the basement of our house is full of clutter, we need to clear it out. Similarly, many people are full of destructive thoughts and emotions.

But how could we ever find out if this is the case with ourselves, if we do not go inside and clear out our basement and explore our destructive thoughts and emotions? Introspection gives us the opportunity to ease our conscience and to free us from our limitations. Emotions and thoughts that limit us always arise from the lower egoism of our personality. Let us seize the opportunity given to us by introspection and set ourselves free from all those limitations, which weight our life down. We then create space for something better and higher in our life. Introspection therefore means an internal exploration of ourselves. We now have the ability to detect the true origins of our emotional and unconscious behavior, and if we then are determined to rearrange our no longer unconscious existence, then we begin to re-create ourselves. If we have made the decision to liberate our true self from the limitations of lower egoism, if "we purify our conscience from dead works" (Heb. 9:14), then we will begin to approach the silent and loving voice of our soul.

Examining and recognizing ourselves is a central task on our journey to self-realization. At least it is for those who are interested in pursuing this path of inner exploration to trace the sources of our emotional and deeper behavior, with the resolve to self-consciously structure our personality and its subconscious parts. The determination to free the self of the limitations of egoism, by releasing "your conscience from dead works" (Heb. 9:14) is moving towards the wise and loving voice of the soul. Daily introspection, also termed 'looking within', is the process of self-examination, of 'knowing thyself'. This is the core practice of every Seeker of Truth and all those interested in self-realization.

My Notes

Chapter 15

The Knowledge about Concentration

*"Learning to focus on your true self will
save you many detours."*

Jens Behrmann

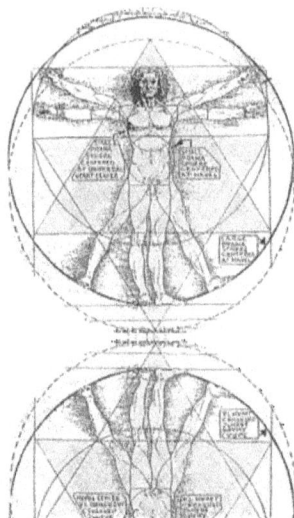

Concentration means that we delve into a matter so deeply that we forget all thoughts and all external influences. We only have one goal on which we focus. In this situation we are this idea, our entire attention is concentrated on this one point and so we focus our entire power. This way, we can work more effectively and without energy loss, and we achieve better results. If we observe children at play or watch them drawing, we can see that they are often so deeply engrossed in their game or their painting, that they no longer perceive outer influences. Being able to completely focus on oneself or on one's goal is a natural and very important ability that is however often lost to us because we are flooded with stimuli throughout the day. We often focus only on the world outside of us and totally forget about the world within us. What attractions may be waiting for us in our inner world? We should therefore continue to develop this ability consciously. The more we focus our thoughts on one point, the less we are distracted. As a result, we are fully aware of the here and now. This is very important for the creation of powerful thought forms. A good example is the Shaolin monks.

They concentrate all their thoughts on an upcoming action such as throwing a needle through a pane of glass. They practice control of their thoughts to a high degree, focus all the energy of their inner being on the upcoming action and then throw the needle with incredible speed onto the glass. To our amazement the needle goes through the glass pane and comes out the other side where it burst a balloon. Through concentration and movement in connection with specific action the most amazing things are possible. We can learn from this example, that the practice of concentrating on a particular point can have resounding results. If we want to increase our ability to concentrate, it is important for each of us to unify our thoughts, which are very complex, so that they become one thought, and allow us to free ourselves from disturbing thoughts at the same time. We should be still within ourselves, so that we can expand our consciousness. This way, a wide spectrum of possibilities will be open to us, perhaps more than currently appears attainable. By concentrating in meditation we will notice very quickly whether our thoughts are destructive or positive. If however we are unfocused in meditation or in our daily life, then we will have great difficulty in reaching the intended goal and we might even fail. Concentration requires a certain amount of effort and thus decreases after a time. This is a normal process. But we can practice our meditation skills (see chapter "Meditation") so that we can hold our focus for a relatively long time. This book also contains an exercise to increase the concentration. With regular use, we can soon learn to concentrate better and keep focused on one point or on a particular action.

My Notes

Chapter 16

The Knowledge about Observation

*"If we do not observe and perceive the little things in life,
how then can we recognize the larger context that arises
from the little things in our life?"*

Jens Behrmann

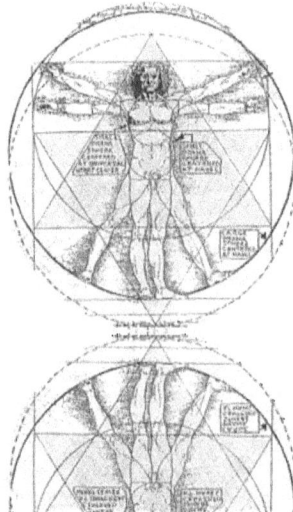

Observation is the focused and attentive perception of situations, circumstances and the environment. We should be able to do this easily and without effort. We should refine the gift of observation more and more. It is a natural condition that every person should make conscious use of. The development of observation is immensely important to our life. Once we have learned to see, without tension, in our memory that which we observed, then we can connect with what is seen and perceived on a completely different level of consciousness.

We can attune to the feelings associated with what is seen. If we refine the gift of observing more and more, we will one day be able to perceive the feelings, thoughts and much more of plants, animals and human beings. We will feel what they feel. Through observation, we can tune in to our environment. Without being conscious of it, we are doing it right now. By attuning to a person, we can feel, for example, what that person feels, what circumstances are at work within him. Observation is associated with concentration.

The following exercise helps to take down barriers in life and to bring about desired changes. Its purpose is to awaken our senses, to develop them and be vigilant.

First, we go to a quiet place either at home, or walking in nature. We then make sure that we are alone or at least will not be disturbed. We sit down quietly for five minutes and breathe. We breathe in for four seconds or four beats and out again in the same rhythm. When we feel that our senses have reached a more conscious state, we get up and start to walk around very slowly and mindfully. We begin to look at everything around us in great detail and we look carefully at the colors, shapes and all the things that surround us.

We try to capture everything around us with all our senses, to feel, see, smell, and perhaps to hear it. We look at everything very carefully and try to find out what kind of connection we could have with it. We take is as much detail as is possible for us and very consciously become familiar with our surroundings. If we are walking, this shouldn't last for more than 15 minutes in the beginning. Then we go back to our starting point and relax again. We now try from our memory to call to life the environment we have just seen and where we gathered so many impressions. We visualize the environment we observed in all its details. We should do this exercise every day to become more and more familiar with our environment. After a few months we are able to consciously remember a lot of details. We can then try to recall events and locations from our past.

We can make them come alive and walk around in them. It may also happen that the past paints its own pictures and we can sit back and relax. In this way, we can expand our consciousness every day and create an accurate picture of situations and circumstances. We now have the ability to perceive details that we would perhaps not otherwise notice. Observation is part of our divine nature. We are fully aware, without the slightest effort.

This is the perfect concentration.

Only in this way do we use our ability to observe everything carefully and in all its detail. Later, we can recall what we observed and so we will also be able to develop an understanding of the divine plan.

Chapter 17

The Knowledge about Contemplation

"We should pay close attention to the path we are walking on, so that we can correct our steps in time"

Jens Behrmann

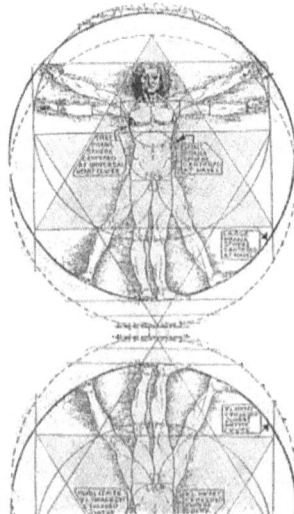

Contemplation (from the Latin contemplare "to look, to consider,") is generally taken to mean tranquility or peaceful contemplation. Roman soothsayers predicted the future by a certain pre-defined area of the sky, the templum (sometimes translated as space for observation), where they observed and interpreted the flight of birds. Similarly on the ground, a sacred space, also called templum, was designated and dedicated to the gods. During contemplari, they observed their sacred spaces (plural templa) in the heavens and on earth together (con means together), and pondered the connection.

Contemplation is also known as a mystical path of Western tradition. As a rule, by living a contemplative life or acting in a contemplative manner, one seeks to obtain a particular state of feeling or of expanded consciousness. A contemplative attitude is determined by calm and gentle attention to a thought and differs from meditation by the fact that meditation seeks to attain total emptiness of spirit. (Source Wikipedia)

Let's take a closer look at the word: "Contemplation

The syllable **con** indicates that something is connected or is brought back together.

The middle part, i.e. the syllable **templ(e)** is an ancient syllable that comes from Sanskrit and means 'measure'. We know 'measure' in many different forms such as speed (it is the measurement of speed) or temperature (the measurement of heat).

The syllable **atio(n)** indicates an action that is repeated constantly, as in: we practice daily introspection.

1. Contemplation is supposed to represent "going inside" the relationship between God and man in the everyday. We bring the divine order into the daily life. We can only find this in our inner being and from there we can align to it.

2. If we want to align to the divine order through introspection, we will realize that our actions should be derived from it. Contemplation is the realization of an action from a position of contemplation.

A contemplative attitude is determined by calmness, inner peace, peace of mind and attention to a particular thought. This means that our decisions and our actions should derive from the stillness and silence that we find in contemplation. This again shows the difference to meditation. Meditation seeks the complete emptiness of mind. As already mentioned, contemplation is also known as a mystical path in Western tradition. Such a contemplative state is described as the achievement of an expanded consciousness. We can achieve this when our thoughts are completely dedicated to a loving God. This is the mystic way of Christianity, which was regarded as very controversial, especially by the church. Mystics were tolerated but were also subject to fierce criticism. Anyone who practices contemplation is on his way to be able to listen to and experience God. The goal of contemplation, then, is to open oneself to the Spirit and the Love of God, to encounter a profound experience of God. Throughout the centuries contemplation has become defined by many clerical personalities. Widely known are Hildegard of Bingen, John of the Cross, Master Eckhardt and Teresa of Avila.

But even today, contemplation is taught by many people all over the world. The church should consider this. Knowledge that comes to us during contemplation is an inner knowing that is not rationally explainable. We may receive answers and solutions to our questions in great clarity, which we would not be able to obtain in any other state of consciousness. But we must learn to distinguish during contemplation that which arises from the imagination of our mind, and that which corresponds to a higher truth.

If there is something that does not feel solid within us and instead feels a bit confused, then it will surely originate from our mind and confuse us rather than bring us clarity. This is how false phenomena of our imagination may show up. They will never be as clear and unambiguous as the true experiences of an expanded consciousness. It is important that we learn to distinguish this for ourselves. We should think of the fact that contemplation is determined by feeling.

There we can experience the amazement, the love and the admiration of the world of the heart. In contemplation, we widen our heart and are able to experience a new feeling or a new aspect of love.

My Notes

Chapter 18

The Knowledge about Meditation

The ending of sorrow is the beginning of wisdom.
Knowledge is always within the shadow of ignorance.
Meditation is freedom from thought and a movement
in the ecstasy of truth. Meditation is explosion
of intelligence.

Krishnamurti

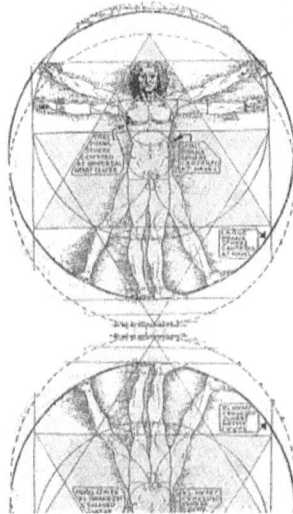

The concept comes from the Latin meditatio and the verb is derived from meditari. It means to ponder, to contemplate, or to think. Which in turn is related to the Latin terms mederi (to heal) and medicina (the art of healing) and the Greek terms μέδομαι μήδομαι (thinking, pondering). Meditation is a spiritual practice performed in many cultures and religions. It takes on a central role in the development of human expanded consciousness. In Eastern cultures it is considered a fundamental and central consciousness-raising exercise. The desired states of consciousness are described differently depending on tradition. Thus, the state attained during meditation will be considered as being at one with all creation or being fully present in the here and now. We can also describe meditation as a time of silence or emptiness. In meditation we turn away from our personalities and the lower egoism to meet the divine aspect of our higher being. Thus we learn to gather and concentrate the spiritual energy or the mind and allow it to work within us. Meditation opens us to receive those deeper truths and wisdom that our personality would be unable to perceive because of our lower selfishness.

We learn by using various exercises, mindfulness, concentration, observation and distinction. If we meditate regularly, this will also have a relaxing effect on our entire system. Therefore, this technique is increasingly being recommended in Western medicine, as it has a measurable effect on our system. Deepening our breathing causes our bodies to relax, our heart rate slows down and we grow calm. Neurologically it is measurable that our brain waves alter. Meditation is very important for introspection, as only in conscious meditation, we can recognize our true self. Thus, in meditation practice it is very important to set yourself a goal.

We should be active and not just passively wait for something.

The mind does not need to be calmed in meditation, because the mind is always calm. What needs to calm down is our personality and the lower emotions, so that the mind can better work within us. That way, we achieve more clarity about the situations we find ourselves in, and therefore our emotions and thoughts, which accompany us in silence. And finally we will be able to recognize whether we should change aspects of our thoughts, emotions or actions. If our lower ego gives more space to our higher self, then we will suddenly feel more love and peace within ourselves. This often changes our perspective on many of the circumstances of our life. Thus, our consciousness expands and in this expanded consciousness, we should very consciously begin to create constructive things for ourselves. Only now can we recognize what controls us and begin to change it and to free ourselves from it. In the beginning, a good meditation should last no longer than 10 to 15 minutes. We should first learn to focus and stay mindful.

If we don't have any experience of meditating, it is possible that we will subconsciously digress and so our meditation turns into an imaginary journey. This can be exciting as well, but it doesn't have anything to do with creating our own reality. If we want to search out destructive thoughts, we should always aspire to the truth during meditation. If we want to create pictures to support us, we concentrate on the correct breathing rhythm and visualize what we want to attain. We draw a beautiful picture and let it grow more and more clear. We let it become real and feel, hear, see and taste it just as if it was real. In a meditation, many things are possible and that which we create will become noticeable in our life sooner or later, provided we concentrate and remain focused on the meditation. We cannot determine a time frame. A lot depends on our personal development and on how we manage to search out restricted thoughts and free ourselves from them. We should get clear that practicing meditation is an intellectual process, in which we search for the illuminated truth and the light. In this manner we will connect with the eternal wisdom, love and intelligence and so can discover much that was hidden within us up until now.

This is what we practice and in the beginning, we may only be able to concentrate for perhaps just a few seconds, and later we can maybe concentrate for one entire minute. Over time we will learn to concentrate better and longer and may be able to concentrate at times for 15 or 30 minutes or even for longer. An exercise to help with this will follow later in this book.

Chapter 19

The Knowledge about Visualization I

*"Imagination is the preview of the
upcoming attractions of life."*

Albert Einstein

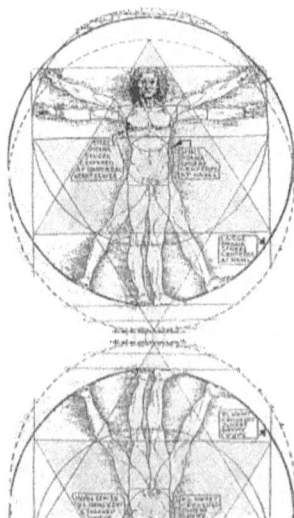

Visualization is applied in sports, politics, business, and in some fields of medicine (including psychotherapy) to achieve better results and to bring about the circumstances that enable these better results. Racing drivers visualize the route and other athletes focus their mind before the performance on that which they want to accomplish. Entrepreneurs imagine in great detail the progressive growth of their company and healers imagine the healing having already taken place. There are many different examples one could state here. This shows us how important visualization is and why it is used for so many individual reasons.

But they all have one thing in common: *They want the outcome to "be successful".*

However, "being successful" can be applied to many different aspects and areas of life. Everyone has his own personal view, perspective and motivation. As described before, visualizing is an exercise that teaches us to concentrate during meditation practice in order to use our thoughts to create crystal clear images before our inner eye. Through visualization, amazing things can happen in us and for us. If we have learned to visualize confidently and with complete concentration, the circumstances in many areas of our life may permanently change. All that now appears unattainable may suddenly come into our experience and become an integral part of our life. We may even be able to enjoy better health. For example, a Polish cellist was able to use visualization to partially heal himself from a paralysis caused by a brain tumor.

After an operation, the doctors had diagnosed a permanent paralysis. As the cellist did not want to accept this as fact, he spent some time practicing visualization exercises while listening to classical music. When the doctors came by again on their rounds, to their great astonishment he was able to move his right leg. After some more time he was even able to give a concert again. Visualization is the language of the universe and the divine. By visualizing we have the opportunity to consciously create mental pictures. To do this, we need to learn to focus completely and to observe. In this way we consciously create thought forms and these support us on different levels until they manifest themselves. We consciously create images, such as the image of the lemon, and we have the ability to create entire paintings. These will be consciously controlled by us and can be very powerful. There is probably nothing more powerful than thoughts, and visualization is the conscious use of our thoughts. This should always be used constructively, and we should never cause any damage by our use of visualization.

It is important for us to understand that this is not about the unconscious creation of a wish; it is not wishful thinking. Wishful thinking is generated by our emotions and is mostly due to external circumstances. This is a thought of desire that we created consciously and deliberately. This thought form was therefore deliberately created by ourselves. It should preferably not originate from our own lower selfishness and lower emotions such as envy, sorrow, hatred etc. Sooner or later this would not be good for us. We will reap what we sow. We should always consider the implications our wishes and desires might have. We should ensure that they are always constructive. That way, we could also use our thought forms to constructively offer help to people in need. Above all, they should not influence the free will of another person. If we consistently perform the exercises in this book, they will help the process of perfecting our concentration and observation so that we can finally be confident in our ability to visualize during meditation. The exercises enable us to learn to create crystal-clear pictures. We should use this ability very wisely, because once created, these thought forms will fulfill our desires. The less we keep thinking about a thought form after we created it, the better it can develop and have an effect. It is better not to create anything we might later stumble over, just because a desire in us was so great that we succumbed to it without due thought. We should always closely examine our desires and wishes so that our desires of today do not become our stumbling blocks of tomorrow.

Chapter 20

The Knowledge about Breathing

"Proper breathing is to us as drinking clear water from a mountain spring in summer. We drink it, we feel refreshed and filled with new vitality."

Jens Behrmann

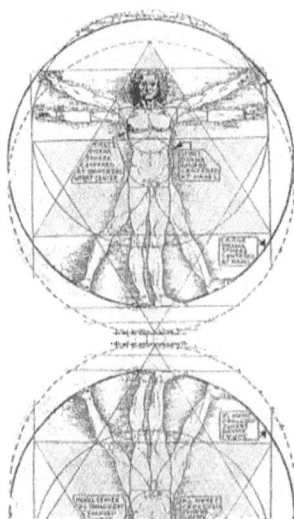

When we are born, we breathe our first breath and in death we breathe our last breath. For all the time in-between, most people are not aware of their breathing and their breathing rhythm. However, the correct breathing rhythm is extremely important. It can make us more balanced; it can lead to greater well-being and improved vitality. Incorrect breathing can actually harm us. If our breaths are flat, we do not take in enough oxygen and therefore we also take in less energy. An entire cultural movement has formed around breathing, and there are so many breathing exercises that one can lose track of them. Something as natural as breathing must be re-cultivated.

One can distinguish between three different types of breathing. Subconscious breathing, which is what most of us do, targeted breathing, and perceptible breathing, which teaches us to experience our breathing consciously in our bodies and perceive it as natural. If we want to alter our breathing rhythm, we should do this very carefully and wisely. Breathing exercises are used and taught in all cultures throughout the world, for example, in therapy, yoga, shamanism, or in many religious ceremonies. Correct breathing should always have a soothing, relaxing and revitalizing effect on our entire system and should stimulate our self-healing powers. This is because when we take in oxygen, we also take in etheric energy.

By breathing consciously, we find our inner balance and we may feel as though we are newly born. If this is not the case, then we certainly do not breathe properly. Mostly we breathe too shallowly. There are many breathing techniques from different cultures, some of them are not so well suited to us Europeans, especially if we have had no special training in conscious breathing. It is important to understand that every person first adopts the customs and traditions of the cultural group he is born into.

Thus, we should first remember the breathing techniques we find in our culture. We should be careful when trying breathing exercises from other cultures, because each person has a very finely balanced nervous system and all is intricately coordinated. If we are overloading ourselves with breathing exercises for which we are not yet ready, we can damage our whole nervous system. In this book, there are some examples to help us find the correct breathing rhythm. The correct breathing rhythm does not overwhelm us, because by consciously breathing and visualization, we can regulate many things. The right breathing is very important for our system. An adult human has more than 50 trillion cells.

All these cells are in communication with each other and should be in balance as much as possible. When cells are out of balance, the entire system may be damaged. If we imagine that every thought, every word and all that we perceive around us as environmental sounds makes our cells vibrate, then we should think very carefully about what influences we expose ourselves to. To enable each of those cells to grow strong, it's important to supply them with oxygen. This happens when we breathe consciously. It's the same with our chakra system. It is a delicate, ethereal system, which should be finely balanced. On the material plane, chakras are discs and on the ethereal plane they are spheres. Each of us has the possibility to keep our chakra system in balance by breathing and visualization. Nowadays there is too much work done with us from the outside. These interventions are usually not necessary and the cleansing of the chakras is very simple. In this book you will find an exercise for chakra purification. Conscious breathing can be used to support holistic or conventional medicine and it works very well. Due to the increased uptake of oxygen, the metabolism and all the organs are stimulated.

The mobility of all muscular hollow organs such as the heart, intestines and blood vessels is stimulated, and blood circulation increases. These positive effects promote healing of physical illnesses. Even muscle spasms can be stopped permanently. In traditional medicine we are familiar with, for example, oxygen therapy.

The following diseases can be positively influenced just by breathing correctly: diseases of the digestive system, diseases of psychosomatic origin and diseases of the cardio-vascular system, panic disorders, burnout syndrome, chronic fatigue syndrome, chronic inflammatory bowel diseases and sleep disorders. There are many more examples, but we can already see how important correct and conscious breathing can be for us.

Chapter 21

The Knowledge about the Heart

*"In a man's heart rests the beginning
and end of all things".*

Tolstoy

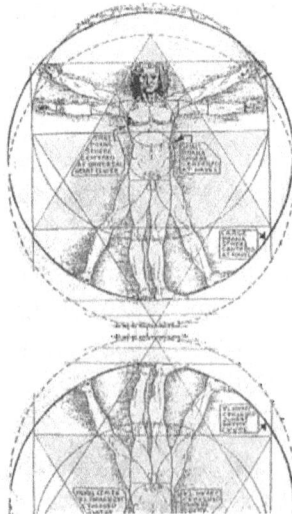

The heart is not only an important organ, it is also the inner spiritual center of every living being. The core of the center is invisible to our eyes. But this is the interface with the higher vibrational worlds. The heart is the spiritual center of our life. Here we find the one true church, which hides nothing and where we can learn all there is to know about our existence. Here is the love that does not judge and does not convict. Here, too, is the gateway to our soul or the needle of the eye that we have to pass through in order to reestablish a conscious connection to our true being.To feel the center of our being, to become aware of it and enter into a conscious connection with it is our main task, because in this center, we will find out many things about ourselves and about real life. It is the interface of the secular with the spiritual, mystical part of our being that we often don't recognize in our daily life.

In the Gospel of Matthew it says:

"Blessed are those who have a pure heart, for they will see God." (Matthew 5.8)

If we find our spiritual heart, we will inevitably experience the joy and the bliss of love that we carry within us.

Before Jesus the Christ left, he gave us one commandment:

"Love one another as I have loved you."
(John 15:12)

This we can only do from the heart and only if we recognize that we will not achieve this unless we discover the spiritual center in our heart. Therefore we should learn to widen our consciousness, because only then will we begin to love our neighbor as Jesus meant us to. For this purpose it is necessary to go within and meditate with confidence. Therefore it is of such importance to have loving and compassionate thoughts. With such thoughts we begin to tread the path to our hearts, to our true being and to the hearts of other people. Without this one love that we find there, everything that we attain is without value.

In First Corinthians, Paul says everything there is to say about this:

"If I speak in the tongues of men or of angels, but do not have love, I am only a resounding gong or a clanging cymbal. If I have the gift of prophecy and can fathom all mysteries and all knowledge, and if I have a faith that can move mountains, but do not have love, I am nothing.

If I give all I possess to the poor and give over my body to hardship that I may boast, but do not have love, I gain nothing. Love is patient, love is kind. It does not envy, it does not boast, it is not proud. It does not dishonor others, it is not self-seeking, it is not easily angered, it keeps no record of wrongs. Love does not delight in evil but rejoices with the truth. It always protects, always trusts, always hopes, always perseveres. Love never fails. But where there are prophecies, they will cease; where there are tongues, they will be stilled; where there is knowledge, it will pass away. For we know in part and we prophesy in part, but when completeness comes, what is in part disappears. When I was a child, I talked like a child I thought like a child, I reasoned like a child. When I became a man, I put the ways of childhood behind me. For now we see only a reflection as in a mirror; then we shall see face to face. Now I know in part; then I shall know fully, even as I am fully known.

And now these three remain:

Faith, Hope and Love, but the greatest of these is "LOVE."

Everything described here we also find in our hearts. The way to get there is by thinking loving, compassionate thoughts. Only if we transform our lower selfishness through our thinking and begin to form a loving character, then we are able to walk the path of the inner heart and conduct our life actions from there. We can resolve to suppress our anger, our rage and our many bad qualities for a time. Nevertheless they will still be there and in due time, they will resurface, because we have not conquered them. We only fool ourselves as well as others, and we are not honest to ourselves.

We need to face up to what is part of us and recognize and transform that within our personality which continues to cause us problems. Then hate is transformed into love, pity into compassion, sorrow into joy, and hostility into friendship. All this will turn us into a person who can be a shining example to others, because he has been transformed from a caterpillar to a butterfly and can now meet his fellow humans with a heart full of love. Only then can we permanently create a world in which everything goes well for ourselves and for everybody else.

My Notes

Chapter 22

The Knowledge about the 3 Bodies

"When you open your eyes and learn to experience consciously through spirit, you will discover that you are more than you now think you are".

Jens Behrmann

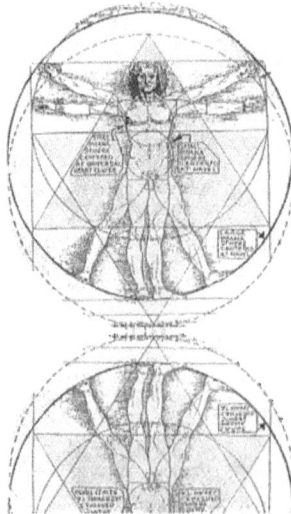

Every human being has three bodies, from the coarse, material body through to the subtle body. These bodies are always interconnected and always infused with etheric energy. Thus, our body and its organs are connected in certain places with our energy centers or chakras.

The first of the three bodies is the coarse, material or physical body. With this body we express ourselves in the material world.

The second one is the psychic or emotional body, where we can find all our emotions and desires.

And finally **the third** one is the mental or subtle body, where we may find not only all of our own mind's thoughts and ideas but also the ideas of different worlds.

All these bodies are interconnected and interact with each other. The physical body is the one we can see. It is always the same in its basic form, no matter whether we are fat or thin. It grows from a seed and an egg cell into an embryo into a mature human being, always following a predetermined plan. However, our thoughts, emotions, feelings and actions greatly affect our physical body. They determine what kind of an expression of ourselves we create. In our emotional body, we find all our thought forms again. They are stored here and from this level they influence us. This manifests itself in our emotions. They are reflected here 1:1. Our approach to the world is affected by our emotions in often crucial ways. Every kind of feeling we have ever felt, be it good or bad, is stored here and from here it impacts on our life. In introspection, we deal with our emotional body and find all those unredeemed feelings and emotions such as anger, jealousy, lack of self-worth, in other words, all kinds of anxiety. Of course, we will also find all our good thought forms here. I have written about this in Chapter one.

What we have created at this level will always come back to the surface until it is redeemed by us. Through our emotional body and the vibrations of light that we produce here, we radiate all that moves us into our environment. So we always create situations and often meet people and circumstances that show us what within us is wanting to be redeemed. This is called resonance. We cannot hold back emotions that are not yet redeemed, therefore we will encounter, for example, lack, again and again, even if in our thoughts we want abundance. But if the light vibration of the thought forms in the emotional body is not a match, the emotional body with its thought forms that we have created ourselves will not permit it. What we consciously or unconsciously radiate as vibration is confirmed. That is why it is so important that we recognize what weighs us down. As is mentioned in the introduction, we need to match the resonance of the light vibration to our desire to be able to fulfill it.

If an opposite resonance is predominant, the desire will remain unfulfilled. Therefore it is of such great importance, that all ideas, with which we create all thought forms in our life, and therefore build the circumstances of our life, are filled with a high degree of clarity, good emotions and clear thinking. They should not arise out of our lower emotions because they will pester us.

Firstly, emotional thought forms are less clear and therefore less powerful, and secondly, unchecked emotions can cause us big trouble. Think of advertisements that directly and specifically appeal to our emotions. Advertisement tries to circumvent our mental power in order to encourage us to buy the advertised product. If this succeeds, we unconsciously act out of an artificially induced emotion that has at worst nothing to do with our own reality.

We are deceived because subconsciously we charge these thought forms with energy and so they begin to work in us. The more people allow this to happen, the more successful the advertised product will be. Our emotions are a very balanced and sensitive system. Everything is coordinated. If we interfere with this system, we should do so very carefully. If we change too much all at once, the entire system might crash. We may improve our character, become more self-determined and then gradually change our entire vibration. In this way, we form a good, solid character that radiates good loving thoughts and lets more light shine through us. If our thoughts are destructive, we darken the expression of ourselves and will continue to wander in the darkness. Because of our lower selfishness we often cannot see the light. Let us now consider our mental body. This is where we find all our thoughts and ideas, and also those from worlds with different vibrations.

Through our mental body, higher wisdom flows into our personality. The more clear our personality, the better we are able to receive. If we have cleaned up our emotional body, we will have clearer reception. The mental body is about receiving higher wisdom and understanding, which are given from this level and which we can incorporate into our life, if we have learnt to notice them. The less we resonate with destructive thought forms, the more our vibrational pattern will be of a higher and wiser truth and the more we will be able to understand ourselves and other people.

All the bodies described here are surrounded and penetrated by the so-called etheric double. Without this etheric double, which has an accurate impression of our physical body at the various levels of life, we could not exist. The etheric double of the material body surrounds us and penetrates us completely and is centered in the middle of each body. On the material level, it stands about 8-12 inches taller than our physical self and psychic people can see the etheric double of the body. All our clothes are included with this etheric double and are reflected at this level. It is in color and you can see through it. Because the etheric double is subtle, most people cannot perceive it.

It is, however, important to know that it exists, because if we want to expand our conscious-ness, we need to know how we can store the etheric energy or vitality, which we need in our life. If we have collected enough energy, it is entirely possible for us to give of this life force, that we take in by, for example, conscious breathing, to others without using up our own energy reserves. We should be careful not to use up our reserves during our work and, where appropriate, take time to recover in between. It does not matter which work we pursue. Life force is good for all of us and it is easy to take it in consciously.

Chapter 23

The Knowledge about Gratitude

"If the word 'thanks' was the only prayer you would ever speak, it would suffice"

Master Eckhart

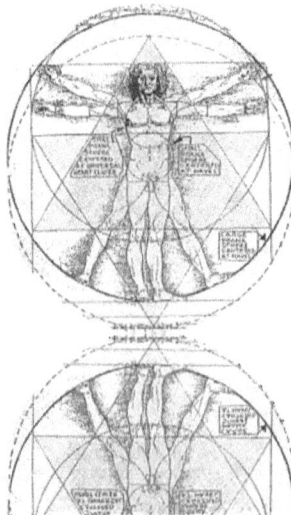

Gratitude is a deep inner attitude towards life and it is a key to greater happiness and peace in our life. We were given the gift of life and with gratitude we appreciate this gift. In many situations we have the opportunity to be grateful. If we have no gratitude within us, we cannot ask what opportunities life has available for us when we find ourselves in a difficult situation. Of course, we can't be thankful for everything that happens in life. There are wars, violence and death, or other things that are not good. But despite of these bad things, we have an opportunity to be grateful every day.

We can be grateful for our food, the fact that we are healthy, have a job, that we are able to provide for ourselves, and much more. If we are aware and grateful, it is much easier for us, when faced with difficult situations where we are not happy, to ask why we might be confronted with this situation. If we are grateful for every good situation in our life, then we can practice to apply this gratitude to all life situations. Gratitude is a tremendous force, through which our life is made even more beautiful and joyous, despite its difficulties. Giving something positive to our life enables us to also make a positive contribution to the world, because we have a grateful attitude and thus can meet other people with greater inner joy. Gratitude should always accompany us, and we should always give it attention. Gratitude has to do with valuing something or someone and opens our heart to the beauty of life. It leads to inner peace and harmony and it opens our eyes. We perceive situations and people in another light and we start to take them as they are. However, we shouldn't be grateful out of self-interest or because we expect that our life will change for the better. Gratitude is, as we said, an inner attitude that has nothing to do with the expectations of our lower mind. If we act out of self-interest, we wouldn't be selfless, but our plans would be driven by lower motivations. Of course this can work, but then we are deluding ourselves and deceiving others. We can be grateful for the past as well as for the present. We cannot be grateful for the future, but if we are grateful for all the situations we encounter in the here and now, we'll create a past full of gratitude that enriches our own life and the life of others. If we are grateful, we feel more pleasure and are happy, and happier people will make the world a better place.

My Notes

Chapter 24

The Knowledge about Joy

Since in the friendship all thoughts, all desires,
all expectations are born without words and shared,
with joy that needs no applause.

Khalil Gibran

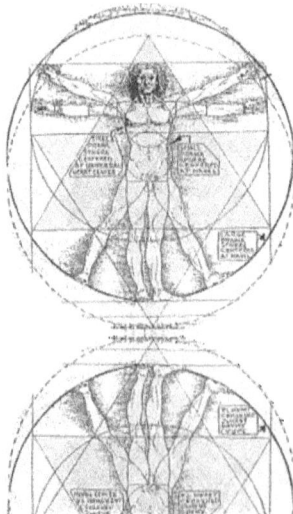

As Friedrich Schiller wrote in his Ode to Joy

Joy, beautiful spark of the gods

Daughter of Elysium,

We enter, drunk with fire,

Heavenly one, your sanctuary!

Your magic reunites

What custom strictly divided.

All men become brothers,

Where your gentle wing rests.

Be embraced, millions!

This kiss for the whole world!

Brothers, above the starry canopy

Must a loving Father dwell.

What more could one possibly say about joy? Schiller said it all. If we could understand the joy with which God created and continues to create everything, and with what joyous enthusiasm the universe and everything we know and not know was created, then maybe we could catch a glimpse of what joy we could be capable of if we would truly include it in our daily life. We all know of tasks that give us great joy.

How enthusiastic and full of perseverance do we pursue our goal and how focused and attentive are we when we enjoy what we do.

But often we don't feel joy when we are faced with a task, instead we do not look forward to it and endure the task rather joylessly, so to speak. As a result, it is no longer easy for us, but it gets increasingly tougher and more difficult for us to do this job.

We begin to grumble and complain more and more and thus ensure that all that could be fun for us is kept well away. Many people spend their entire life like that. Their daily tasks fill them with less and less joy and their life is more and more steeped in sorrow, misfortune, grief and sadness - in a word, joylessness. Their whole life will over time become increasingly joyless and they will radiate this joylessness, at all levels of their being. This is certainly not the right way to lead a life full of joy and happiness. It is certainly not always easy to fulfill our duties with great joy. But it is important to understand that the more joyfully we approach the tasks assigned to us, the more joy there will be in us. We then build a light vibration of joy within us and around us.

What will have to happen as a result?

The responsibilities that fall to me will bit by bit become easier to handle and will feel more in tune with me. As the saying goes: As above so below, as below so above. This is the law of resonance and through our inner attitude we work with this law.

It enables us to create more joy, because we recognize and release all those conflicts within us. As a result, our environment will change alongside us. Gradually, the less popular work, tasks or circumstances in our life will become less.

Tasks or circumstances in all areas of our life will improve and will suit us better. This illustrates the importance of joy and our inner attitude towards that which we encounter at work, within the family and in all other areas of our life. Enjoying what we do makes us stronger. If we can ignite this joy within us, we will then be able to give the gift of joy to ourselves as well as to others. Joy makes us feel good, because with joy, our personal needs are meet. This is one of the greatest gifts of all. We can receive more joy through self-knowledge and a good way of life. Joy can permeate many areas of our life and transform our expression of ourselves. Joy is the expression and the result of a deep gratitude.

Chapter 25

The Knowledge about Humility

"I cannot understand how humility exists, or can exist, without love, or love without humility"

Teresa of Avila

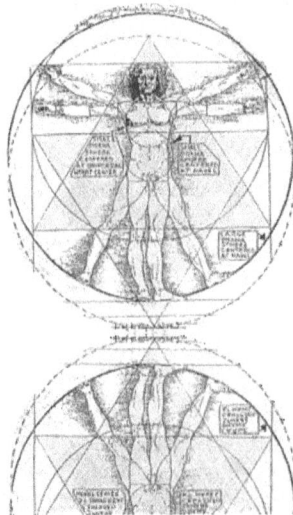

Humility could be described as the willingness of individuals to defer their own personal needs and wants, by their own free choice, in favor of the will of God and for the service of their fellow men. In other words, it is the attitude of a person who wants to be of service. In the Christian sense, it refers to the attitude of accepting external circumstances without complaint, because one recognizes them as the will of God, which has not yet been revealed to us. Humble people trustingly accept any circumstances whatsoever. According to many Christian mystics, humility is a prerequisite for a Christian life and a prerequisite for completely overcoming one's self and attaining true peace, and so being able to look at our fellow humans in a different way.

Guided by simplicity and purity, we will find the nature of God in every living being. Humility plays a central role in many faiths. Only when all our efforts are associated with humility, do we live with God's blessing. Jesus the Christ and many of his apostles are examples of humility. Jesus was full of humility and prayed for his enemies in spite of adverse circumstances and his knowledge that they wanted to kill him. At the hour of his crucifixion, he asked forgiveness for the sins of his enemies and those who persecuted him. If we want to believe what is written, we can see that all the apostles were martyred. They all followed their faith and a deep inner attitude of humility toward Jesus Christ and God.

This is how the apostles are said to have died:

1. John

John is the most beloved of the disciples of Jesus the Christ. With one word, he destroyed the temple at Ephesus, and is said to have re-awakened its dead priests to life. In Rome, he survives being immersed in boiling oil and is exiled to Patmos, where he wrote the Apocalypse. In A.D. 100 or 101 he is requested to either perform a heathen sacrifice or drink poison. He chooses death.

2. Bartholomew

Bartholomew goes on missionary journeys to Egypt, India, Asia Minor, Mesopotamia and Armenia. There, he converts the king, whose brother subsequently orders the apostle to be tortured to death. He is skinned alive. His skull is kept at the St. Bartholomew's Church in Frankfurt.

3. James

James the Younger is the first bishop of Jerusalem. He converts many Jews and goes on missionary journeys through the Holy Land. He argues with Paul about his intention to proclaim the Word of God to the gentiles, too, but he cannot stop him. By order of the Jewish high priest Ananus, the Apostle is thrown off the temple Easter A.D. 62.

4. Peter

He heals the sick, raises the dead, and travels through Asia Minor and Greece to Rome. For 25 years, he is the first pope. In A.D. 64 or 67 he, like many other Christians under Emperor Nero, is nailed to the cross head down, out of reverence, as he does not want to suffer the same death as Jesus. His grave is at St. Peter's Basilica.

5. Matthias

Judas, according to the story we know, committed suicide after he betrayed Jesus Christ. His successor is Matthias. He evangelizes in Judea, then in Ethiopia, where he accomplishes many miracles. In A.D. 63, Matthias is beheaded by heathens, with a hatchet. His remains are buried in Trier - the only apostle's grave on German ground.

6. Andrew

The brother of Peter, Andrew preaches the Gospel, especially to the wild Scythians in southern Russia. He works many miracles and is crucified because he converts the wife of the Roman governor Aegeas in Greece. Since out of reverence he does not want to die in the same way as Jesus Christ, he is crucified on an x-shaped cross. This x-shaped cross is now known as the St. Andrew's cross.

7. Thomas

Thomas evangelizes in Syria and Iran and then moves to India. He baptizes the three Magi and by torture a high priest tries to force him to perform a sacrifice to an idol. Thomas speaks to the idol, and it melts away immediately. This makes the high priest so angry that he runs his sword through him. His remains lie in Ortona on the Adriatic.

8. Matthew

Matthew leaves Palestine about A.D. 42. He writes his Gospel as a messenger of faith, traveling through Persia and Ethiopia, where he defeats the sorcerers Zaro and Arphaxat and converts some of the royal family. His opponents arrange for him to be killed by sword. His remains rest in Salerno since the 10th century.

9. Philip

Philip preaches for twenty years to equestrian nomads in the southern Russian steppes. He is said to have tamed a dragon in the temple of the Roman war god Mars by holding a cross up to it. In A.D. 87 he is crucified in Hierapolis (the modern town of Pamukkale in Turkey). His remains are still venerated in the church of Dodici Apostoli ("Twelve Apostles") in Rome.

10. James the Elder

James the Elder is a missionary in Spain. He then returns to Jerusalem, where he dies Easter A.D. 44. He is said to be the first Apostle to have died a martyr's death. He is beheaded with the sword by order of King Herod Agrippa. His remains lie in Santiago de Compostela, which is a place of pilgrimage that still attracts millions of pilgrims.

11. Judas Thaddeus

Judas Thaddeus goes to Edessa (now Urfa/Turkey), preaches in Syria, Mesopotamia, Phoenicia Armenia, and, together with his brother Simon the Zealot, in Persia. There, both of them are tortured to death by priest of Mithras. They are delivered from their suffering by being clubbed to death. The remains of the martyr rest at St. Peter's Basilica.

12. Simon the Zealot

Simon the Zealot evangelizes predominantly among those Jews who do not live in the Holy Land. Together with his brother Jude Thaddeus he travels through Persia. In the city of Suanir (the ancient Colchis on the Black Sea) he is sawn in half by priests of the Iranian god Mithras. His remains lie in Rome, Cologne and Bad Hersfeld.

They were all killed, just as Jesus the Christ had foretold.

So what does this mean for us? Should we also die a martyr's death? No, but certainly many of us suffer a little every day in ways that we impose on ourselves.

How? Yes indeed, I speak of our lower selfishness that brings about suffering.

Why?

Because our lower egoism is often not humble but proud, and creates all kind of circumstances in order to gain an advantage.

There will be no respect for other people, for the environment and for the creatures that live in it. We only need to open our eyes to what happens locally, or to look at the Third World. This will show us what is lacking in our society, namely love and compassion. We co-created a world, which is concerned with power and material benefits for the individual or for a few corporations at the expense of the world's populations. I cannot see any humility here, or any love or compassion, and certainly not the true love talked about by Jesus the Christ. If every single person would realize that the world has enough resources for all of us, without disadvantages to any one of us and then we would be able to create a world free of oppression that resulted from selfish, individually directed personal motives.

Together we could do so much more than we can imagine right now. Even though there is still some way to go, we can start right now. We should be aware that our prosperity exists at a high cost to many other people. There is a lot of arrogance around these days that I fear would be hard to surpass.

Compassion? Yes, but ... Humility? Yes, but...

It is clear that the whole world cannot change from one day to the next. But we do have the opportunity to start with ourselves and regard our neighbors with more humility, more respect and above all, more love and compassion. This will cause a whole lot of change.

When will you start?

My Notes

Chapter 26

The Knowledge how to work with
Thought Forms

*"Herein lies the root of all joy and all suffering,
that has ever existed and exists "*

Jens Behrmann

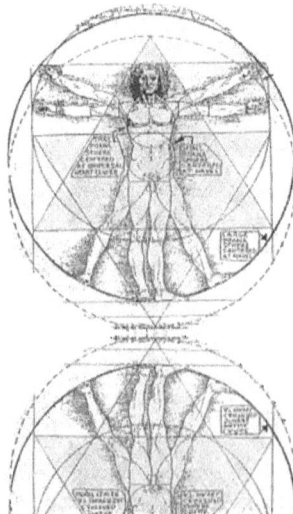

Everything we think and feel and radiate therefore, creates a thought form. They are living beings and live a life of their own, entirely independent from who created them. Most people are not able to perceive these kinds of living entities, and thus they do not know anything of their existence. We are able to distinguish two types of thought forms.

1. Those that might arise out of a desire, so from an emotion, these we call wishful thoughts.

2. The thought forms that we create with our mind consciously. This thought form we call a thought desire.

Every person sends out, through their thoughts and feelings, a vibration and in that way, they determine exactly, the type and quality of the vibration of their thought forms. There are usually feelings that influence a person's life, this person is certainly more emotional and is under the influence of his desire. So thinking within us at these moments takes a secondary role. We act out of our emotions. When a human being is guided by very destructive emotions, it can easily take him into trouble.

An example:

Someone begins to play cards. At first, he may play just for fun. Maybe he wins a little and then he loses a little again. If he wins he feels good, if he loses he feels bad, and wants to win back the lost money.

Or, it's just the lost feeling of victory?

So then, the cycle of emotions runs its course, and he loses many more times, more and more money. He begins lying to people, he borrows money from friends because the bank account is already overdrawn and he may even begin to steal. He is trapped within his own destructive emotions and thoughts, and so he begins to create more and more of the same; poorer living conditions for himself, and all that he loves. Had it been just a game, his life might have been different, because he would have created other emotions and thoughts.

If he had given a thought to the consequences of his action, he might have been able to remain conscious, so then he would certainly have acted differently. His emotions were not able to take him into this situation. So dangerous can our emotions be, as they have a big impact on our lives. They let us act without thinking, and then one could say that we are delivered to our emotions.

If a man can stand largely under the influence of his thinking, he will much more likely avoid such situations.

This does not mean that we should not have any emotions. But we need to learn to control our emotions and not allow our emotions to control us. This is only possible once we realize that really, everything we think and feel, creates a lively thought form, and this will have an impact on our behavior.

"There is nothing in our human existence, within everything that we experience, without such a thought form".

The thought form lets us experience"

This is why you might want to think carefully about what it is that you want to generate thoughts on how you would like to live your life. In order to create a satisfied and happy life for yourself and for others, you should practice producing good and powerful thought forms.

This can be achieved by means of visualization, which are themselves composed of strong and clear thoughts. All unreasonable wishes and desires should take only a minor role.

Then, all thought wishes are consciously created for the task for which they were intended and will help bring about fulfillment a lot faster. These types of though forms are stronger and live much longer. Ordinary people, who have not mastered these process's, produce more thought-forms from their lower emotions and desires, and often become "slaves" to the wishes which have been produced in this way. Each thought form generated, returns back to its creator. This is a natural law.

Everyone can certainly recall that he was suddenly reminded of something specific. This increases the thought forms, by reason of our memories back into our consciousness. This cycle repeats itself until this thought forms succeeds, in the area of the subconscious of man where it resides in larger duration. And so we provide them with energy from our etheric double and so the life of the thought forms extends.

As already mentioned, in this way we form our habits, addictions such as smoking, drinking, etc. Sooner or later a person will be faced with the thought forms that they have consciously or unconsciously created.

Very powerful thought forms can even force people to realize the desire from which they were created. Every aspect of our personality and all the circumstances connected with it, are the sum of the thought forms that we have created, consciously or unconsciously. All thought forms are created from the same substance, as we are and indeed the whole universe is, consists of etheric energy. Since we have created them, they then belong to us and remain with us until they have fulfilled the wish and purpose for which they were created for.

How do we create a thought form?

To create something, we must first have the desire to do so. If we are unaware of how to, then it should be possible for us by just beginning to desire? Men like cars, and so when they see a car, it can create a strong desire in them to possess this car. A strong desire arises, which will follow purposely on how to be able to own this car. In order to subject matter, a series of thought-forms arise, whose ultimate goal is attainment of the car for the person who created and sent them. Awareness of this process and the desire to get to know it or to own it, alone are not sufficient. Further thoughts must follow, so that such a thought form can be created. So you begin the process of subconscious visualizing. Therefore, it is concentration and craving, which creates images in us, and these images consist of energy.

Is thinking not more as the condensation of energy?

The internal process of Life is nothing more than to receive impressions and to interpret them. How we perceive the world, therefore depends on the type of thought-forms, which we produce and direct back outwards. Nothing in the outside world can have a value for us when we have no equivalent inside.

"That which has value in us, gives value to everything that is outside of us. As within, so without. Everything is within us"

When creating a thought form, the image of this appears within our perception and is projected forward, into the area of the brow chakra at the bridge of the nose, this is located between the eyebrows. It then leaves the etheric system of our human form and assumes its own natural form. It continues to move within the mental levels and it starts a cycle, and the strength of this cycle depends on the underlying craving. In any case, it is destined to return back to the person who created it in the first instance. We can notice when we suddenly recall it again. This is in any case the created thought form by us.

Thought-forms tend to dominate people, since they are not even aware of them. Indeed, most people do not even know what a thought form is. In some cases they can even gain so much power that we do not have any control over it. So people become slaves to their desires.

"Now that you know what a thought form is, this will benefit you in successfully creating a better life"

My Notes

Chapter 27

The Knowledge about taking Action

*"It does not help to be a good person
if you do nothing!"*

Buddha

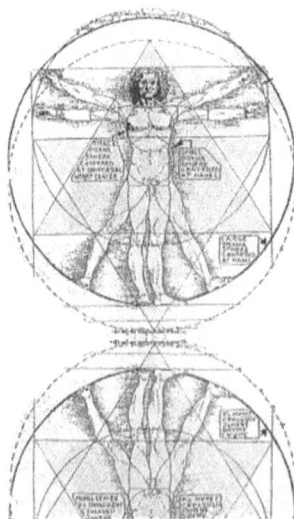

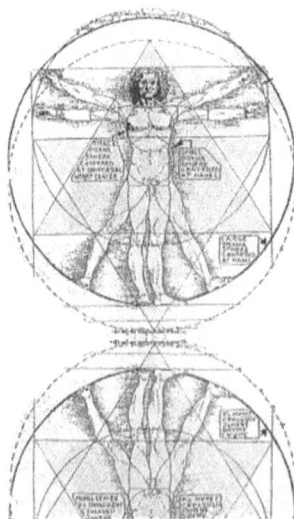168

Everything we have read so far has now settled inside of us and gives us an idea of how we can change our life. However, up until now this has only been theoretical. Reading and thinking remain theory, until we begin to take action. Only then will we be able to make use of the opportunities that present themselves to us. Where we encounter an opportunity, it is important to examine it carefully and then act appropriately. We cannot wait for something to happen. We need to take action ourselves. The more we have thought about our actions and the more we are sure about the actions we carry out, the better our results.

With all the important actions we should first tune into ourselves, so that we can become aware of the consequences our actions may have for ourselves and others. What are our motives, what options do we have and why do we want to act like this and not in different ways? Are we sure that we won't hurt anybody, not even ourselves? If all those questions are answered, we need wait no more. We do of course need to choose the right time for our actions. A bad choice of time can nullify everything in one moment. Then, although maybe we had good intentions, the timing was not chosen carefully enough. Sometimes we need to wait for the right time, which is not always easy.

A good example is buying a brand new car. Many people buy a car when the time is not right. But they are already emotionally attached to their desire and emotion, they are driven by their desire: this car, I must have it now. The timing may not be good, but they think that somehow it'll be all right. Then they buy or lease the object of their desire, even though they know that the timing is unfortunate. But emotion is stronger than reason. So now they have the car and are kind of happy about it, but then again, not really happy, because they know that they have not acted properly. They have acted against their inner wisdom and that now gives them a guilty conscience. Our soul or our higher self communicates with us in this way. It shows itself quite often in a guilty conscience resulting from our misdirected actions, even if we have not yet performed them. We should learn to listen to our inner voice. Similarly, it encourages us when we are doing something that's right. We then have a consistently good feeling about our intention. Emotional thoughts can disturb us and guide our action in the wrong direction. They can harm us and even harm our life. We can observe this every day all over the world. But we should first concentrate on ourselves and observe whether we fail to do the right thing. It's not always easy to act properly, in whatever circumstances. However, to learn all this and to go into the silence inside to check whether everything is on track is absolutely the right way to clear all obstacles in our life. We should certainly listen to our conscience, our inner voice, and be guided by it. Above all, we should act accordingly. If we do not, it will eventually have unpleasant consequences for us and maybe for other people, too.

We throw a stone into the water and we can watch the waves ripple out across the surface of the water, in all directions. Everything is in motion, and even the calm water a little way off is affected. The larger the stone we throw into the water, the greater the energy of the impact and the farther the waves will travel. The energy that results from our thinking and our action also causes such waves rippling out in all directions. We often cannot see this immediately. However, everyone should question of what quality the waves are that ripple out due to his thoughts and actions.

To sum it up:

Taking good action = clear and proper thinking + good intentions + inner awareness + right time = good results and the creation of good emotions for ourselves. **We have created a thought desire.**

Taking bad action = wrong emotions determine our thinking + unclear thinking + wrong intentions + no inner awareness + wrong time = bad and the creation of bad emotions for ourselves. **We have created wishful thought.**

This applies to all areas of our life.

As the old saying goes: Our thoughts are free.

Yes that's true, but are they free from our own lower selfishness?

How to recognize this and if necessary to free ourselves of it, can be found on the following pages. They are intended to let the lower selfishness of our personality grow smaller, so that our true self can take up more space within us and so become what we express in our life. Thus we will feel more peace, more love and more happiness.

My Notes

Chapter 28

The Knowledge about the Exercises

"Exercise is not as important as practicing.
The practitioner should be practicing an exercise."

Jens Behrmann

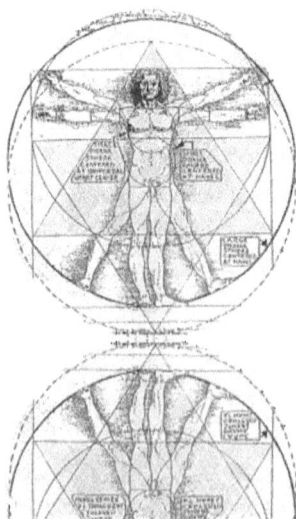

Finding the right breathing rhythm

It is very important for us to find the right breathing rhythm. As described in the chapter on breathing, our breathing helps us to feel enlightened and to be healthier because we receive more energy. Thus, breathing is one of the best ways to learn more about ourselves. For each exercise described here, three-quarters of the belly should be filled with air, then three-quarters of the lungs should be filled with air. Following this, we fill the entire belly with air, then the entire lungs. There are many different breathing rhythms and they all have their validity. They all have the goal of supporting the practitioner.

We want to practice the following rhythms:

Rhythm 4:4

Rhythm 6:6

Rhythm 8:8

Rhythm 12:12 or longer

We practice breathing the 4:4 rhythm until it has become easy for us and we have grown accustomed to it. Next, we practice the 6:6 or the 8:8 rhythm, until we have found the rhythm that is right for us. Everyone has a different breathing rhythm, and therefore we should do these exercises until we feel comfortable with them.

These breathing exercises are very important because they form the basis for many subsequent exercises.

A basic meditation

we create a sphere of light to surround us

We should always start an exercise with this meditation, which enables us to leave the worries of everyday life behind so that we can become centered again. We should create this sphere of light every morning and every evening. It is thought that this sphere makes us less permeable for other people's thoughts. In addition, it enables us to be well protected, wherever we are, and prevents us from losing any energy we need for ourselves. We can perform this exercise in the morning, before we start the day. We breathe the 4:4 rhythm and relax our body. We let all emotions become calm. Now, with every breath we take, we allow a white sphere of light to form within our belly.

Every time we inhale, this sphere grows larger and brighter. With every out-breath we let go of all thoughts of worry and grief and all that burdens us. Every time we inhale, the sphere of light continues to grow larger, until it surrounds and penetrates our body completely, like an oval shell. Now, we breathe in the white light from this shell and exhale all the stressful thoughts and emotions. We consciously breathe like this for five minutes. In this way, we free ourselves from stressful thoughts and feelings. We can start the day centered and strengthened and end the day in such a way, too.

Finding the silence in ourselves

We breathe deeply and relax. We breathe in a rhythm that suits us. We let go of all thoughts; all the stresses of everyday life don't matter now. Our whole being focuses more and more inwardly. All the sounds of our surroundings no longer affect us and we only pay attention to our breathing. Slowly, we focus on our heart. We feel how it beats and keeps our body alive. It beats with the precision of clockwork. Each beat brings us closer to our heart. Our thoughts and our whole consciousness depend on our heart.

We feel the presence, the peace and tranquility that come from our heart. Nothing can unsettle us now. If possible, we should spend 10 - 15 minutes concentration on this silence and then slowly come back to reality. Even though at the beginning we will not be able to focus on our heart for so long, we should not get discouraged and continue to practice. Only then will we learn to focus for longer and experience real silence within us.

Practicing forgiveness and finding peace

Practicing forgiveness and finding peace are probably two of the most important qualities that one can acquire. If we cannot forgive, we remain tied to people and situations. We are not free, and so can find no peace. Finding peace is very important to avoid being thrown off track by feelings while meditating. Therefore, is of great importance that we should behave with loving kindness in all situations we find ourselves in. If we are at peace with ourselves, within ourselves and with other people, never mind the circumstances, then we give a valuable new dimension to our life.

Beginning with a basic meditation, we sit or lie down comfortably. All thoughts that come will go again. Bit by bit we let go of all thoughts. Everyday life and all that concerned us today loses its importance. We relax more and more. When we are relaxed, we begin to breathe the 4:4 rhythm. With every breath, we exhale everything that disturbs us. We feel increasingly comfortable and concentrate on our breathing. With every breath we let a sphere of white light grow within our belly. Everything dark leaves us when we exhale and disappears into the atmosphere. The white, bright light of the sphere gets bigger and surrounds us and gradually permeates us. We breathe deeply and calmly in our rhythm. Now we visualize a pink sphere within our chest. It keeps growing bigger and bigger, until at the level of our chest cavity it completely surrounds and permeates us. It has the size of a basketball. We feel calm and peaceful within ourselves. Then we begin to visualize an image. We are walking through a meadow of beautiful, bright flowers. It's a wonderful day.

It is warm and the sky is blue. In the distance we can see the ocean and hear the sound of the waves.

Maybe we can even smell the sea. We walk on and we see a beautiful beach; we walk toward it. After a while we reach the beach, lie on the sand and look at the ocean. It is the color of turquoise. We lie on the beach and the sun warms our skin. We feel the warm wind in our hair, we feel safe and relaxed. After a while we decide to swim in the calm, clear water.

We get up and walk slowly into the pleasantly warm water, until we are immersed in it and begin to swim. Swimming is easy for us and while swimming we can see the ocean floor.

That's how clear the water is that we swim in. We might even see some fish, sea turtles or dolphins. All the inhabitants of the sea are friendly towards us. We swim farther out and we feel more comfortable and secure than we have in a long time. After a while we decide to turn around in the water and look back at the beach, where we see one or more people. We cannot yet recognize them, but we have a feeling that we know these people. We decide to swim back to the beach. Bit by bit we come closer, until we feel the ground under our feet and can leave the water. Now we can tell that we know these people. They are those with whom we had disputes, and maybe also those who were not well disposed towards us, or even have harmed us. Perhaps there are also people we were not well disposed towards and whom we have harmed. Nevertheless, we now meet with love and full of understanding. We smile at each other and look lovingly into each other's eyes, embrace and forgive everything we have done to each other and whatever it is that has led to disagreements between us. It feels good and it is a wonderful relief.

If we see more people on this beach, then we repeat the same with them. We forgive whatever we have done to each other.

When we are finished, we once again go to the ocean. We look out at the sea that lies calm and clear before us. The sun reflects in it and we can see our own reflection in the water. Now we realize that we should forgive ourselves, too, for everything. We love and forgive ourselves now, just as sympathetically as we forgave our fellow men.

We recognize that we too bear responsibility for the conflicts and sorrow we experience with each other. Once we have forgiven ourselves, we look once more into the clear and bright blue sky and we truly enjoy this moment. Then we take the opportunity to fill ourselves fully with the energy of the sun.

When we feel that we are completely filled, we go back to the meadow behind the beach. We go back across the lawn and remind ourselves of the pink sphere full of love. We are now back at this level. We begin to feel the sensations of our body, the legs, arms and then the whole body. Slowly, at our own pace, we arrive back in our body, open our eyes and are again fully present in our surroundings.

Balancing our three bodies

by creating blue, pink and golden spheres

We select a quiet place at home or in nature, where we won't be disturbed, and we begin to relax and breathe in the rhythm that is right for us. We can feel our body in its entirety. Now we focus our attention on our toes. We feel as though all of our attention is in our toes. We are our toes. Then we move on to our feet. Once we can feel them as we did the toes, we move on to the ankles, calves and then to the knees. We then feel the entire lower legs, the knees, calves, ankles, the soles of the feet and toes, everything together. We take a deep breath, then another one.

We feel comfortable and secure. Now we move consciously on, up through the body. From the thighs we move on to the abdomen, to the pelvis and up to the solar plexus. We feel the energy and it now takes the shape of a sky-blue sphere. We begin to perceive more and more clearly this loving and powerful sky-blue energy that we take into our solar plexus on the physical plane. With every inhalation it becomes more defined and shines ever brighter. This sphere fills our solar plexus, and it permeates and surrounds us to a distance of some 12 inches. While exhaling, we leave all thoughts of fear behind. All that is dark, and any doubts we have leave this sphere with each exhalation, so that it is always bright and clear blue as the sky. We wish that all living things now experience good health for their material bodies. We move on to the chest. Here we perceive a luminous, light pink color. It comes straight from our heart center and spreads out as a pink sphere of light.

All emotions and desires are silenced within us. We are completely concentrated on our heart center and the pink sphere of light that expands ever further. It grows as large as the blue sphere.

Where they meet, the colors of the spheres don't mix. Here too, we breathe out all that is dark and stressful from this sphere until it consists only of a very clear light pink. The sphere of light stretches farther and farther until it surrounds the entire planet, and we wish for love, inner peace and joy for ourselves and for all living beings. Then we proceed to our head, where we create a golden sun in the form of a light sphere and repeat the visualization as with the other two spheres. All dark thoughts leave us now. There are only creative and loving thoughts for us. We wish for understanding and peace of mind for all living beings. In the beginning, we do this exercise for 5 – 10 minutes, but later, we can extend this time. We take a deep breath and while exhaling, we arrive back in our body and are fully present again.

Revitalizing the body and its organs

At the beginning, it is helpful to select a quiet and comfortable place where we will not be disturbed. Later, after some practice, it may be possible for us to meditate even in a noisy environment, because we will remain firmly focused on ourselves. It does not matter whether we lie or sit down.

We slowly begin to relax. We breathe in quietly and evenly and exhale equally calmly and evenly again. We let go of the worries and stresses of today and yesterday. We relax our body and let our thoughts and all our outer senses come to rest. We breathe quietly and evenly in our own rhythm. We now start to breathe in through our nose for four heartbeats or four seconds. First we breathe into the belly and then into the chest, so that we fill belly and chest with our breath. Then we breathe out in the same rhythm. First we empty the belly, then the chest cavity until both are completely empty. Now we begin to concentrate on feeling our toes. We focus only on our toes. Once we can feel our toes, we move on to the soles of our feet. Here we pause for a moment, then move on to the ankles and to the calves.

We feel these very intensely and then move our focus to the knees. Now we concentrate on feeling our entire lower legs - the knees, calves, ankles, the soles of the feet and toes. And there we pause for a moment. Then we move on to the thighs and feel them very intensely. We move on to the hips, feel the connection of legs and hips. Now we focus on the entire lower body and imagine how this is wrapped in a bright white light and is suffused by it. Then we move on to the abdomen where we feel all the organs that are located there: bladder, kidneys, liver, intestines, spleen, gall bladder, etc. We see how all these organs are imbued with a radiant white light. Now we move on to our solar plexus and feel the energy that is there. We breathe a bright white light into our solar plexus for a few minutes. We are well and relaxed and feel how we are charging up with energy. We flood all the internal organs of our lower body with this brilliant white light - the bladder, the stomach and kidneys, etc. We now concentrate on our chest. We flood all the organs located there with the brilliant white light - the heart, lungs, diaphragm, etc.

Then we move on to the thyroid gland. It consists of two parallel lobes that look like a butterfly. We usually don't notice the thyroid gland, because it is tiny in comparison to the other organs. It has its seat in front of the neck, below the larynx. We flood the thyroid with the brilliant white light and notice how good it feels. Then we move on to our shoulders, feel those, then feel the upper arms, elbows, forearms, wrists, and finally both our hands with all their fingers. With our inner eyes we see that the area around thyroid gland, shoulders and arms down to the solar plexus is surrounded by a sky-blue light. Once we have realized this, we go back to the thyroid gland and from there move up the neck to the head.

We feel the larynx, the lower and upper jaw, teeth, tongue, the uvula, the mouth with its lips, the nose, ears, eyes, forehead, the brain with all that is within it, and

finally the entire head. Here, too, we let this bright white light fully penetrate the entire area. We feel comfortably relaxed. Now we look at our entire body. It is wrapped in white light from the feet up to the head. We sit like this for a few minutes, then come back again to the material world at our own pace.

Filling up with etheric energy

We choose a place where we can be alone. If this is not possible, we can still do the exercise. We sit or lie down comfortably and relax, while leaving all emotions behind and letting our thoughts come to rest. Then we begin to breathe in the 4:4 rhythm, filling first the belly then the lungs with air, emptying first the belly then the lungs as we exhale. After a few minutes we begin to focus on the solar plexus. We can collect and store life energy in the solar plexus.

With every breath we now take, we create a sky-blue sphere of light in the solar plexus. The sphere gets bigger with every breath until it completely fills the solar plexus area right down to our genitals. The sky-blue light shines ever brighter and brighter. All dark spots within the blue sphere are expelled when we exhale. After a few minutes, we focus on our solar plexus again and from here begin to channel life force into our etheric double. We envision this double as a transparent double of our body. It looks just like us and wears the clothes we wear. We imagine that we are completely suffused and surrounded by this transparent body, then consciously fill it with life energy. We see how the etheric body is filled with more and more life energy. We do this for about five minutes. Then we're done. It is important to practice this exercise daily. After a while, it gets easier to become charged with life energy.

The Heart

the center of our being

The heart is where our divine and human aspects unite. We sit or lie down comfortably. We let go of all stressful thoughts and free ourselves from our everyday cares. Then we begin to breathe in the 4:4 rhythm. We then focus on our toes. First we feel only the toes of our right foot, then those of the left foot. Then we feel the soles of both feet and once we are able to do this, we continue to the ankles. Then we feel both feet in their entirety - the ankles, the soles and the toes. Then we focus on our knees and move on to the thighs and the pelvis. We feel the hips and our internal organs.

We are comfortable and relaxed. We become lighter and lighter. We then focus on the solar plexus. We feel the energy that is located in it. We pause for a moment, then move on to the chest. We feel how our lungs are working perfectly. Our chest is moving up and down in perfect rhythm. We breathe in and out. Breathing is very easy now and we feel very well. We move to the thyroid gland, then on to the shoulders. We feel the shoulders, then the upper arms, elbows, forearms, wrists, and finally all the fingers of both hands. Then we move back to our shoulders. From there we proceed up to the neck and on to the head. We feel the lower jaw, mouth, teeth, tongue, cheeks, upper jaw, nose, eyes, ears, forehead, perhaps even our hair. Then we move on into our brain. From here we see how the whole body is wrapped in and penetrated by a bright white light. With every breath, we breathe in this white light. We do this twelve times. We then focus on our heart. This is where, with every breath, we create a pink sphere of light. This gets bigger and bigger with each breath until finally it completely suffuses us at chest level surrounding us to a distance of some 12 inches. We keep our attention focused within this beautiful pink sphere of light. It is connected with our heart. We sense into it and feel the love that it contains. We see this center as the center of our earthly and spiritual being. We feel how great a force is emanating from this center, we are flooded with love, and realize that everything we seek can be found here. Now we let the love we feel spread throughout ourselves.

It spreads out over our entire body, spreads into the room we are in, continues through the entire building and the surrounding area, then the love continues to spread out over our home town and even further through the whole country, through the whole planet and all living beings that dwell on it. Everyone who is receptive to this love will receive it now. We wish love and inner peace to all creatures. We then return slowly back into the pink sphere. We feel our body again, all our limbs, we stretch our arms and legs. We come back to this reality and open our eyes. This exercise helps us and all creatures on earth to feel more love and joy. It is important that we always let other people decide for themselves whether they want to accept this love or not. We can only make it available. If someone does not want it, we should respect that.

Every person develops in his own time and if we influence another person by our actions, even if our intentions are good, it may be that he is prevented from an important experience, which may disrupt his own learning process. We may hinder him with our good intentions.

The detection of destructive thought forms and emotions

This exercise is meant to track down our stressful emotions and thought forms and remove them from our emotional body. If we suffer from fears, anger, phobias or addictions, this exercise helps to let go of these emotions and thought forms that constantly influence us. It is important that what we detect during the exercise is replaced with something positive. To this end, we imagine that we create a white sphere of light that has the qualities we want to have in our life instead of the destructive ones we currently have. We can also write these qualities on or into this sphere.

For example, we can replace enmity with friendship, or self-doubt with self-esteem, hatred with love, etc. We can ask God to bless the sphere and declare that it may not interfere with our free will. This is especially important if we want to do something for other people. We create the white sphere, equip it with the chosen quality, let it be blessed by God and declare that it will not interfere with the free will of whomever it is intended for. Then we send it to the person for whom it is intended. If this person is not ready for it, the quality impressed on the sphere will still be a light impression in his aura. When the right time has come for this human being to want to develop this property for himself, the impression will support him and help him move forward faster. We start with the basic meditation. We imagine that with each inhalation a white sphere is formed in our belly. With each inhalation this white sphere grows bigger. With each exhalation we breathe out through our mouth all the darkness that may be inside. With each breath, the white sphere of light gets bigger until it completely penetrates and engulfs us.

It surrounds us like an oval shell and suffuses our whole body and surrounds us to a distance of about 12 inches around the body.

We breathe quietly, we feel very well and supported. All our thoughts are silenced. Every thought calms down within us. Our attention is focused on inhaling and exhaling. Now that it's become very silent within us, we begin to feel the emotions that come to the surface. We observe closely and concentrate on the emotions that are there now. We allow any feeling to come to the surface and look at it as we would look at an image. When we find a destructive feeling, we simply swap it for a constructive one that will support us from now on in. Then we begin to feel our body, our toes, legs, abdomen and upper body, head and arms and fingers. We feel whole again, and return from the meditation.

What has happened?

Emotions that burden us even though we don't realize we have them, are unconscious thought forms at work within us, which unconsciously define a part of our actions in daily life. Many people speak of so-called beliefs or doctrines. They are perceivable for us and once we become aware of them, we then have the opportunity to work on them to change things within us, so we can build the foundation for something better, which we know will be constructive and support us positively.

Cleansing the seven chakras in the material realm

This exercise is meant to cleanse our chakras on the physical level. The three chakras we have worked with so far are located on the etheric plane. Many cultures know them as the energy centers. Knowledge about the chakras is found in ancient Vedic scriptures. The word chakra is Sanskrit meaning wheel or circle. Psychics can see the chakras in a round shape like a flower. On the physical level of our body, there are seven major chakras. These are associated with energy channels. The chakras have different colors and functions.

These we will consider in this book in a limited way. It is important to know that they exist and that we have the possibility to purify them from pollution. The seven chakras are located along the front of our body. They have different attributes, functions and colors that I will briefly describe here. For the purpose of this book, it is only important to know where the chakras are located and what functions they have.

1. **The Root Chakra**

    Its color is a bright red, it represents our basic trust and it is located at the base of the coccyx.

2. **The Sacral Chakra**

    Its color is a bright orange. It represents our sexuality, our enthusiasm and creativity and is located about an inch below the navel.

3. **The Solar Plexus Chakra**

    Its color is a bright yellow. It represents energy, will and wisdom and is located at the solar plexus.

4. **The Heart Chakra**

    Its color is bright green, it is sometimes seen as bright pink and represents our ability to love.

5. **The Throat Chakra**

    Its color is bright blue, it represents our communication with the outside world.

6. **The Third Eye Chakra**

    Its color is bright indigo and it represents our expanded perception of the things that our physical eyes cannot perceive.

7. **The Vertex or Crown Chakra**

Its color is white or sometimes purple, and it represents our spirituality and the universal connection with our highest consciousness.

Now for the practice:

We breathe in our basic rhythm. All thoughts and emotions come to rest. We focus entirely on our body. We feel our feet, lower legs, knees, thighs, our pelvis - we linger here a moment - then we move on to the abdomen, the chest cavity, the thyroid and from there on to the shoulders. From here we proceed to the upper arms, the elbows, then on to the forearms, wrists and hands. We stay here for a moment. Then we move up to the neck and to the head. We visualize how the bright white light spreads across our body. It begins in our abdomen and spreads with every breath from the inside outward in all directions. It then radiates beyond our physical body by about 12 inches all around. With every in-breath we inhale the brilliant white light and with every out-breath we exhale everything that burdens us. When we are surrounded by this perfect sphere of light and feel secure and calm, we then focus on our root chakra.

We see how it rotates and see its bright red color. If we can detect dark spots there, they are ejected with each rotation of the chakra and released into the environment.

We do this until the chakra radiates only in its own color. We do not have to worry about anything. We do the same with the other chakras. When we have finished, we come all the way back into the here and now.

Clearing other people's destructive thought forms

We breathe in our basic rhythm. All thoughts and emotions come to rest. Silence is spreading within us. We breathe deeply, with each inhaling and exhaling we feel more relaxed and quiet. We focus on the center of our heart and stay there for a few minutes with the questions: Who am I? Am I life itself or am I an expression of life? Can I acknowledge that I am not life itself and that the body that gives me expression is not me, but I use it as a vessel for my spirit?

With the heart we can see the truth. We think about that in this meditation and we begin by talking to the heart. Again, we begin by breathing deeply and focusing on the body. Is our body in a state of equilibrium and is it feeling well? We flood the body with more and more bright white light from the solar plexus. It spreads throughout the body. Each cell is flooded and surrounded with light until the light suffuses and engulfs us completely. It forms an oval shell that radiates around the body to a distance of about 12 inches. We bathe in the soothing feeling of comfort and love. All thoughts grow quiet and we feel great peace. Now it is time for us to free ourselves from other people's destructive thought forms. No thought forms from other people may influence us and then limit our free will. We are masters of our own destiny and responsible for our own thoughts, feelings and actions. No other person may influence us in a destructive manner, or bind us against our will.

In thought or out loud we speak the following words:

"All destructive thought forms from other personalities that influence my personality, must leave my personality now."

Then we come back from meditation into the here and now. Perhaps we notice a change in us, but it is not important if we don't.

We can rest assured that all the thought forms that do not belong to us have left us now. We have received a gift from God: Free will.

No being may influence this free will if we do not allow it.

Visualization

Observing and drawing from memory

For this exercise, we need a household object from our household such as a cup, and some paper and a pen. A pencil would be good, but we can use any type of pen. We take the cup in our hands and look at it very closely. With this exercise, we are trying to look at this item so intensely that we remember all its details. What shape is the cup? What color? Does it have a handle? How is it shaped? We feel the material in our hands. How does it feel?

Bit by bit, we commit to memory the exact shape of the cup, the color, maybe it has small cracks or is a little chipped. We memorize everything. When we are finished, we put the cup aside. Now we close our eyes and begin to imagine the cup in every detail - every little detail. We create an image that reflects the cup in all its details. When we have done this, we open our eyes, take paper and pen and draw the cup from memory. If we can't draw well, that's okay. We draw as well as we can. We repeat this exercise again and again, until we have the perfect cup drawn from memory. We visualize the image of a mountain meadow.

The following exercise has already been described previously in this book. It is about a setting in the mountains that we create within ourselves, by visualization.

We breathe evenly in our basic rhythm and let all thoughts and emotions come to rest. It's a bright summery day and we are in a meadow surrounded by beautiful mountains. We sit down in the grass. In our mind, we furnish this meadow with lush green grass and lots of colorful flowers.

We see butterflies, birds and bees. We look at the bright blue summer sky, where no clouds are to be seen. We notice how a bird circles in the sky and we observe its elegant flight. On our skin, we feel a warm summer breeze and we feel comfortable and secure. We now turn our eyes back on to the meadow. We lie down and take in all the many different smells, the smells of grass, flowers and trees. By and by, we become aware of all kind of sounds. In the distance, we can hear a gurgling mountain stream. We are now looking across the meadow and discover a horse grazing peacefully in the distance. We look at it carefully: what color is the horse? How big is it? We notice everything in all its detail. Then, we turn our attention to the mountain stream. We decide to go there. We walk through the meadow and we notice that we are barefoot. Our bare feet touch the grass. How does that feel? Maybe the grass is tickling the soles of our feet.We look at everything around us in great detail on our way to the mountain stream and memorize everything carefully. After a short walk we reach the stream. It flows calmly and we sit comfortably on its banks. The stream has a very calming effect on us. It is so clear that we can see right through to the ground. Perhaps we discover some fish or we see dragonflies reflected on the water. In the distance, we hear the bleating of new lambs, we see them running playfully across the meadow. We notice such lightness and joy within us as we observe this beautiful place. After a while we decide to return to the meadow. When we get back to where we started from, we look across the entire landscape that we created, and we feel how all is filled with peace and harmony. We can always return to this place. Here we find rest and inner peace. If we wish, this peace and harmony can spread from here throughout the whole world. Now feel yourself gradually returning to your body and come back to the here and now.

The deliberate creation
of a thought - form

Before we begin this meditation, it should be emphasized again that we should use conscious visualization only for our own good. We should not use it to satisfy lower needs, or to influence other people for selfish motives. I would like to point out once again that we should not let our desires and longings of today become our rocky path of tomorrow.

We start with the basic meditation

We let go of all thoughts and situations of daily life. It does not matter whether they are good or bad. We feel safe and we relax more and more. Our feelings come to rest and now have no effect on us. We breathe deeply and let arise in our mind's eye a glowing picture of our desire. We fill the picture with more life force that we take in through our breathing and pass on to the picture. The picture is becoming clearer and more colorful and luminous. We want to paint a perfect picture in all its details. Everybody should visualize the image of what now appears most important to him. If we succeed, we can imagine ourselves entering this picture and starting to walk around in it. Now try to observe yourself, as you walk around in this multi-dimensional image.

See the colors, hear the noise, maybe you can perceive the smells. After that, let the image be flooded with your positive emotions. Then we can ask God to bless our image. If we have created an image for another person, the purpose of the image can only be fulfilled if it does not suppress the free will of whomever it was created for. We can repeat this whole procedure a few times until we feel that it is complete.

We should then give this self-created mental image no more attention, because once created it takes time to develop.

Perhaps we completely forget the image we created and end up surprised when we no longer expect it. In any case, we have created an image that exists and is alive. It will fulfill itself sooner or later. If we are not yet skilled in visualizing, it may not be easy for us, and we can instead write the essence of our wish into the sphere. We can also do this if we have a wish for others.

Finale

I now wish many new and good experiences to everyone who uses these practices, and hope that he himself may come a bit closer to his own true self and the truth that is in each one of us as "The Knowledge". I also hope that new and better ways of looking at situations may open up for you. That way, more light will enter into the life of many people, who in turn will radiate this light themselves. Thus we will have more love, compassion and understanding for ourselves and for our neighbors, for all of nature and for the entire creation of God with all its beings.

In Love and Gratitude,

Jens

About the Author:

Jens Behrmann was born in February 1964. His spiritual journey included some amazing experiences. One day, his consciousness suddenly expanded so much that he found himself on the sphere where the archangel reside. He could feel the infinite love, for which we as humans have no words, not in any of the languages that exist in this world. You must experience it and then you'll know it. He knew in a split second that this love was different from any love that he had ever felt. Several times he visited Israel because he was told to go there by the Council in his dreams.

There he followed in the footsteps of Jesus Christ. During these visits he had several experiences that ushered in profound changes in his life, including that it was allowed him to give healings at the place where the Last Supper took place. He himself says that God heals, not him. Today he is an author, workshop leader, gives lectures and healings.

For more information about Jens, his lectures, workshops and readings, go to: www.the-knoledge.info